Understanding the Artificial Intelligence Revolution

After many years during which it languished in relative obscurity, in remote classrooms of computer science departments and in small prototype projects for tech companies, artificial intelligence (AI) is now a searingly hot topic across the media. Yet much of the public discussion is so feverish that an understanding of the basic scientific and engineering elements of the field is easily lost, often resulting in exaggerated claims, as well as dangerously neglected threats.

This concise and sober book presents a brief history of AI, explaining in clear language the central engineering innovations that have produced the current revolution. It distinguishes between imagined dangers and the very real problems that AI is creating. Spread across seven short and accessible chapters, this book explains the developments behind deep learning and the applications of deep neural networks (DNNs). It addresses both the imagined and actual risks posed by the AI revolution, before outlining the elements of a rational public policy on AI, covering topics like tech monopolies, disinformation, bias, hate speech, intellectual property rights, and inequality.

Suitable for the general reader, *Understanding the Artificial Intelligence Revolution: Between Catastrophe and Utopia* is the ideal book for anyone seeking a clear and informed introduction to AI.

Understanding the Artificial Intelligence Revolution
Between Catastrophe and Utopia

Shalom Lappin

CRC Press
Taylor & Francis Group
Boca Raton London New York

CRC Press is an imprint of the
Taylor & Francis Group, an **informa** business

Designed cover image: Better Images of AI

First edition published 2025
by CRC Press
2385 NW Executive Center Drive, Suite 320, Boca Raton FL 33431

and by CRC Press
4 Park Square, Milton Park, Abingdon, Oxon, OX14 4RN

CRC Press is an imprint of Taylor & Francis Group, LLC

ISBN: 9781041036685 (hbk)
ISBN: 9781041035077 (pbk)
ISBN: 9781003624790 (ebk)

DOI: 10.1201/9781003624790

Typeset in Minion
by codeMantra

To my sweet little granddaughter Nina, who entered the world smiling and continues to do so, brightening everything around her

---

Contents

Preface

I HAVE WORKED IN THE natural language processing domain of AI over the past 35 years, and its problems have occupied most of my professional life. During this time, my children have asked me on many occasions to explain what I do in my research, in terms that are clear and interesting. They were invariably dissatisfied with my answers, finding them both obscure and evasive. They were entirely right. This book is, at least in part, an attempt to pay off the explanatory debt which I still owe them and which my grandchildren can now lay claim to. It is also an attempt to put the remarkably rapid pace of progress in AI in some historical perspective and to consider its social and economic aspects.

AI is now a hot topic in the media. This is a recent development, after many years during which it languished in relative obscurity in the more remote classrooms of computer science departments and in small prototype projects of tech companies. Much of the public discussion is feverish and not informed by an understanding of the basic scientific and engineering elements of the field. This results in hyperbolic claims, groundless euphoria, unmotivated fears, and dangerously neglected threats. In this book, I have tried to strike a balance between including sufficient technical content to provide a sense of how current AI systems operate, while remaining accessible to a general audience. I have also devoted a major part of this book to distinguishing between imagined dangers of AI and the very real problems that it is creating. The latter pose serious questions of public policy, many of which have gone unaddressed. I attempt to raise these and to look at possible solutions.

I am particularly grateful to my son Yoni for pressing me to write this book, for several years, despite my stubbornly resisting. It is thanks to his prodding that I finally gave in and produced it. I would also like to thank numerous friends and colleagues for helpful discussion of the ideas presented here and useful comments on earlier drafts. These include Scott

Aaronson, Devdatt Dubhashi, Haim Dubossarsky, Hector Geffner, Pat Healey, Sharid Loáiciga, Ian Malcolm, Mori Rimon, Haim Rubinstein, Nicholas Sims-Williams, and Moshe Vardi. Elliott Morsia, my editor at Taylor & Francis, has provided invaluable advice and support. I bear sole responsibility for the views expressed and for any errors that remain. My wife, Elena, my children, Miriam, Yaakov, Yoni, and Shira, and my grand-children, Zohar, Ela, Omri, Galia, Noam, Ido, and Nina, were always there for me with love, fun, therapeutic teasing, and good humour.

Some of the research presented in this monograph was supported by grant 2014-39 from the Swedish Research Council, which funds the Centre for Linguistic Theory and Studies in Probability (CLASP) in the Department of Philosophy, Linguistics, and Theory of Science at the University of Gothenburg.

I presented the main ideas of this book in a series of three lectures sponsored by the School of Electronic Engineering and Computer Science at Queen Mary University of London in October–November 2024. Many thanks to Roz Cresswell, Hayley Cork, and Aurelie Leroy for organising this event and publicising it. I am grateful to the audiences of these lectures for their comments and feedback. I gave talks on neuro-symbolic models in AI to the Chalmers Data Science and AI Seminar, and the CLASP Seminar, in February 2025. I thank the audiences of these talks for helpul discussion, which helped to clarify my thinking on this issue.

Shalom Lappin
London
March 2025

Author Biography

Shalom Lappin is Professor of Natural Language Processing in the School of Electronic Engineering and Computer Science at Queen Mary, University of London; scientific researcher in CLASP at the University of Gothenburg; and Emeritus Professor of Computational Linguistics in Informatics at King's College London. He is also a fellow of the British Academy and a member of the Academia Europaea.

CHAPTER 1

The Early Years

1.1 INTRODUCTION

When I was a (comparatively) young research scientist in the artificial intelligence (AI) Department of the IBM Thomas J. Watson Research Center in Westchester County, New York, in the late 1980s and the early 1990s, many AI projects were under threat of reduction and, in some cases, closure. It is difficult to imagine this today in the heady environment in which AI enjoys near universal fascination and major investment. The dominance of AI in computer science and industry is a fairly recent phenomenon, stretching only over the past two decades. Prior to 2000 the fortunes of AI waxed and waned in a series of cycles, moving from the heights of optimism (AI spring) to the troughs of scepticism (AI winter). There were several extended periods when work in AI was subjected to sharp funding cuts, large tech companies closed down their AI projects, and universities relegated AI to a secondary area of research and teaching. We are now in the midst of a blossoming AI spring.

While at IBM Research I had the privilege to come into contact with colleagues like Fred Jelinek and the members of his speech and language group, who were working on highly innovative statistical models of natural language processing (NLP). These models were in the process of revolutionising the methods used in AI, particularly in the areas of speech recognition, machine translation, and syntactic analysis. They helped to lay the foundations for some of the developments that subsequently transformed the field into the vibrant domain that it has become. At the time, I was heavily invested in more traditional symbolic methods and rule-based approaches to NLP. I did not appreciate the full power and

DOI: 10.1201/9781003624790-1

potential of the new models. Looking back on this period and reviewing some of the work that I had resisted, I now wish that I had been more receptive at the time to the innovations that were taking place in machine learning applied to tasks in AI.

AI has become a big business. The Stanford University Human-Centered Artificial Intelligence (HAI) *Artificial Intelligence Index Report* for 2023 states that global private investment in AI for 2022 was $91.9 billion (US).[1] Although this was a decrease of 26.1% relative to 2021, it was an increase of 18 times the amount of private investment in this area in 2013. The report also notes that since 2014 the focus of research in AI has shifted from universities to tech companies. In 2022, these companies produced 32 significant machine learning models, while academic institutions created only 3.

AI is a major area of scientific research and engineering. Its products and its development have become a focus for mainstream media attention and intense public discussion. Some of this discussion veers into hyperbolic praise of AI's technical achievements and possible applications. It portrays these in ecstatic terms, as offering solutions to many of our deepest social and economic problems. Other opinion paints an apocalyptic view of the dangers that it poses. It regards AI as a dire threat to human survival and autonomy. Much commentary of both types is not grounded in a clear understanding of how different AI systems work and what they can actually do.

In this book, I will try to clarify how current AI systems operate, and I will look at their capabilities. I will try to distinguish the real from the imaginary dangers of AI. On the basis of this distinction, I will consider some of the elements that a rational public policy on AI technology should include, if its benefits are to be fully realised, while its risks are effectively constrained.

Chapter 1 presents a brief history of the field. This is a history that is frequently overlooked in contemporary discussions of AI. As a fast-paced area of science and engineering, we tend to erase our past with each new generation. It is important to recall the earlier experiments and systems out of which the achievements of the present have emerged. The pattern of development is far from linear. It exhibits many twists, turns, and unfruitful leads that did not turn out. Conversely, ideas that were once nearly discarded later returned in revised form to animate successful approaches.

In Chapter 2, I describe the deep learning revolution that produced current AI models over the past 15 years. This came in two waves. The first consisted of various types of Recurrent Neural Networks (RNNs) and Convolutional Neural Networks (CNNs). The second arrived with the creation of transformers, which support large language models (LLMs).

Chapters 1 and 2 contain some technical material, which is unavoidable if one is to understand how AI systems function. I have tried to minimise the formal aspects of the discussion by banishing formulas and equations to footnotes, with references giving pointers to full explanations. Mathematical concepts, AI system diagrams, and scientific terms are all accompanied by informal explanations. I am hoping that these are sufficient to guide readers unfamiliar with ideas in computer science through this part of the exposition without too much discomfort. The remaining four chapters are largely free of detailed technical content, but they do rely on a general understanding of the models introduced in the first two chapters.

Chapter 3 is devoted to a tour of several of the applications that AI offers now. These indicate some of the important benefits that we derive from these devices. They constitute the ways in which AI is changing the environment that we live and work in. As should become clear in this chapter, it can indeed be a source of social and economic benefit.

Some of the more dramatically imagined dangers of AI are the subject of Chapter 4. In particular, the idea that we are about to fall victim to the imminent rise of super intelligent artificial agents that will threaten human survival is, I argue, far-fetched. It is not grounded in either the actual capabilities of current systems or technologies we are likely to develop in the foreseeable future. It also relies on several problematic and largely unmotivated ideas on the emergence of general intelligence from complex electrical circuits.

AI does, however, carry very real threats of serious damage, some of which have already come clearly into view. It is necessary to recognise precisely what these threats are if we are to avoid, or at least constrain, this damage. I take these issues up in Chapter 5.

Chapter 6 is devoted to exploring how we might best maximise the benefits while controlling the risks of AI through the instruments of public policy. The main issues that I address here are which aspects of AI require government regulation and what might a workable regulatory regime look like. This is a pressing political and social question in which everyone has a strong interest.

Chapter 7 summarises the main arguments of the book. It draws several conclusions on the current trends shaping work in AI, and it suggests directions for pursuing some of the issues raised in the previous chapters.

1.2 INTELLIGENT MACHINES

AI emerged at the dawn of electronic digital computing. The British mathematician Alan Turing played a central role in establishing the theoretical foundations of both the theory of computing and of AI. Turing (1936) presented the first formalised model of a system for programming a device to compute the values of certain mathematical expressions. His abstract machines determine the values of functions of a certain type, computable functions.

In slightly more technical detail, Turing machines define the class of computable functions. A function $f(x)$ is computable if and only if there exists a precise procedure (an algorithm) such that, for every argument x for which f is defined, the procedure determines the value of f for x in a finite number of steps. Turing's model consists of a class of simple abstract machines (Turing machines) with an unbounded tape of paper and a writing head that can mark the tape with a symbol at each stage of a computation. The tape moves back and forth in each direction. If it halts in a finite number of moves and yields a defined answer for each argument that was its initial input, that function is Turing computable. The class of Turing computable functions is the class of computable functions. Turing machines follow programs that encode algorithms. They provide a mathematical model of a computer (although computers have finite, rather than infinite storage facilities).

During the Second World War, Turing worked on code breaking as a member of the legendary Bletchley Park team. Their decryption machine was a programmable electronic calculating device that anticipated modern digital computers. After the war, he published a paper that had a substantial impact on the development of AI. Turing (1950) proposed a heuristic criterion for deciding if a computer has intelligence of the kind that one attributes to humans. He described a set-up in which a person communicates with a computer by keyboard, with the device concealed behind a curtain. He suggested that if, after an extended conversation, the person cannot distinguish the device from a person, then we can infer that it has demonstrated intelligence on a human level. This experiment came to be known as the Turing test, and it was widely (but by no means universally) accepted as a reasonable criterion for attributing general intelligence to a computer.[2] With the recent success of LLMs in generating natural dialogue responses to human queries and comments, the plausibility of the Turing test is very much open to question. I will return to this and related questions in Chapter 2.

In the 1950s, the United States became the centre for work in AI and computer science generally. The major founding event of AI research took place in the summer of 1956, when the American computer scientist John McCarthy organised a summer workshop at Dartmouth College entitled Dartmouth Summer Research Project on Artificial Intelligence. The forum lasted for several weeks, and it included well-known researchers from computer science and several other disciplines, including psychology, statistics, mathematics, neuroscience, and electrical engineering. It featured the participation of some leading figures in these domains, such as Marvin Minsky and Claude Shannon. The Dartmouth workshop was a defining event for AI. It shaped it as an interdisciplinary field in which patterns of learning, cognition, and reasoning are modelled through systems that run as programs on computers.

In thinking about the development of AI, it is useful to distinguish two approaches. Strong AI seeks to build a computational model of general human intelligence. To the extent that this venture is successful, it will create devices that are capable of the full range of abilities involved in human learning and cognition. These will involve, among other capacities, acquiring native fluency in a natural language, the ability to engage in unrestricted dialogue, recognition of different types of objects and events in the world, reasoning about these objects and events, rational planning, inference from premises to conclusions, and estimation of the probability of events based on available evidence. From a cognitive perspective, such an artificial agent will be at least as competent as a human to perform tasks that require human intelligence.

The second approach, weak AI, seeks to build systems that achieve (at least) human levels of performance for specific tasks and applications. It is not directed at developing a machine that exhibits general human intelligence. In fact, almost all the progress made in AI to date has been of this second kind. Artificial agents now outperform humans in games like chess and Go. They power expert systems in law and medicine. NLP programs turn spoken speech into text, and they support machine translation. AI computer vision recognises faces and classifies objects. When combined with NLP, it generates descriptions of images and answers questions about the objects in them.

It is hardly accidental that most progress in AI has been task and application specific. We are able to explore specific human cognitive abilities, and we can construct precise computational models of them. We can test these models against the performance levels of people for these tasks. By contrast, it is not clear that strong AI posits a realisable goal. We do not have a clear understanding of general human intelligence, nor is it obvious that we ever will. We can recognise intelligent behaviour in humans, but we have no sense of what a scientific theory of general human intelligence would look like. It is precisely for this reason that Turing chose to approach the question of whether computers can achieve human intelligence by proposing a criterion for identifying when a device is behaving intelligently, rather than by attempting to characterise general intelligence.

I will return to the issue of strong AI and general intelligence in Chapter 4. It has figured prominently in some of the more extreme views about the threat that AI poses to human well-being. However, for the most part, I will be focussing on the work done within the framework of weak AI. It is this perspective that has shaped AI through most of its history, and it continues to remain dominant in the field today.

1.3 METHODS AND STRANDS: NEURAL NETWORKS

From the earliest period of AI, researchers experimented with a variety of methods for representing the processes involved in acquiring and using knowledge. These tended to fall into three broad categories. One stream of work employs neural networks, which were initially inspired by attempts to construct abstract models of the brain. A second uses symbolic formalisms to encode information and operations applied to it. The third approach relies on statistical methods to reason about the probability and uncertainty of events. Distinct strands emerged within each of these approaches to specify separate research programs centred on particular theoretical orientations and domains of application.[3]

McColloch and Pitts (1943) presented the first formalised model of a neural network. Their neurons are information processing units that take binary inputs in the form of 0 and 1. They have activation functions for these inputs that cause them to produce binary outputs. The units correspond to the truth functions (logic gates) of propositional logic. Networks of these neurons can be used to encode computable functions.

Rosenblatt (1957, 1959) introduced the perceptron, which became the foundation for work on learning with neural networks.[4] It consists of a neuron that receives inputs $x_1,\ldots,x_n$ to which weights are assigned. These weights are summed, and a weighted bias b is added to the sum. This bias corresponds to background activation noise. This information is passed to a binary activation function φ, which determines whether to produce a positive output y if the total summed weights are above a threshold, and 0

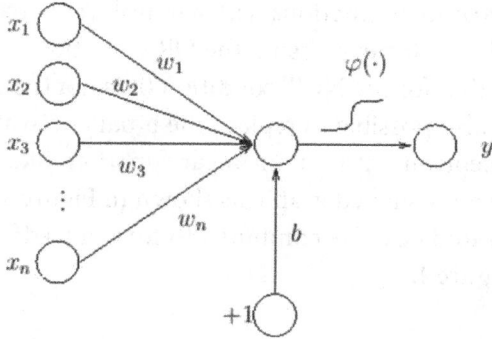

FIGURE 1.1   The Rosenblatt perceptron. From Honkela (2001).

otherwise. The value of b is learned from the data on which the perceptron is trained.

The structure of the Rosenblatt perceptron is given in Figure 1.1. Rosenblatt's perceptrons were able to learn binary classifications of objects into categories. In one of the first demonstrations of this learning task, he trained a perceptron to distinguish programming cards marked with symbols on the left from those that had symbols on the right.

These neural units are organised into networks that compute the values of functions. An important limitation of Rosenblatt perceptrons is that they can only compute linear functions. The values of linear functions are represented by a straight line on a graph.

Perceptrons were inspired by neurons in the brain. Their inputs were intended to correspond to the signals that neurons receive from sensory and other sources. The weights that they are assigned reflect their relative importance in activating operations that generate the brain's output representations. While modelling the brain's informational patterns was a significant concern in the initial years of neural networks, the relationship between these patterns and contemporary networks is now taken to be an abstract analogy by most researchers in AI. The design and operation of a neural network is determined, for the most part, by computational concerns, rather than by an interest in modelling brain activity.

Minsky and Papert (1969) show that a Rosenblatt perceptron cannot learn non-linear functions. One of their examples is the Boolean exclusive *or* function, XOR, which holds of arguments A and B if either A or B is the case, but not both. Exclusive disjunctions figure in many real-world alternatives. So, for example, one can turn left or right at an intersection, but not both left and right. Although single perceptrons cannot encode XOR, it is possible to learn such functions with a multilayer perceptron network. It has one set of layers for expressing the OR condition (either A holds or B holds), and another for the NOT condition (it is not the case that both A and B hold). It is also possible to replace the binary activation function in a Rosenblatt perceptron with a non-linear function, like sigmoid, whose values determine an S-shaped graph, as shown in Figure 1.2.

Layers of such units can be combined to form a feedforward network, represented in Figure 1.3.

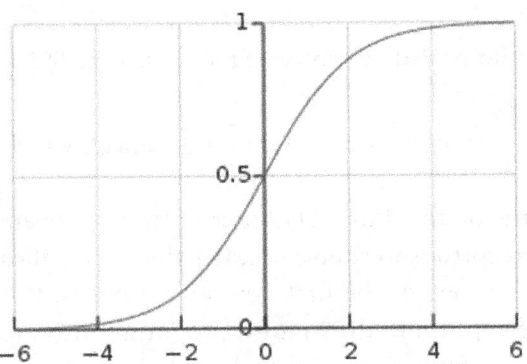

FIGURE 1.2   Sigmoid function.

Source: Reproduced in Lappin (2021).

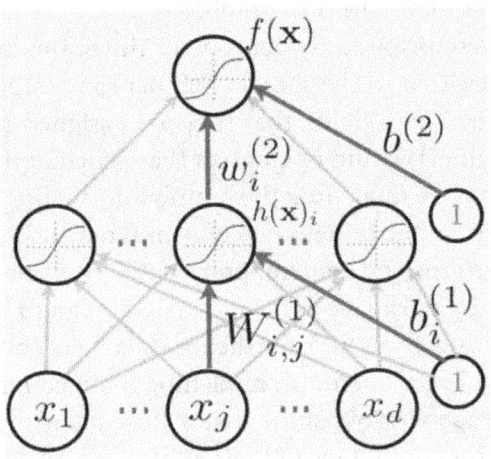

FIGURE 1.3   Multilayer feedforward neural network with sigmoid activation functions. From Gupta (2017).

Source: Reproduced in Lappin (2021).

Neural networks of this kind are trained by initially setting the weights for their inputs as random values, and then incrementally correcting them against the data on which they are trained. The error rate of the network's output is calculated as the gradient (angle) of a loss function. This involves minimising the distance between the network's output and the data to which it is exposed. Training involves proceeding down the slope of the function by incremental correction until a statistically estimated optimal point is reached. This procedure is referred to as *stochastic gradient descent*. It is generally applied in tandem with *backpropagation*, which involves feeding the difference between the desired and the actual output of the network backwards along the connections among the units, in order to calculate updates for the weights of the inputs. The approach of using neural networks to build classifiers and to estimate the probability of events came to be known as the connectionist school of AI.[5]

Simple multilayer feedforward networks achieved considerable success in a variety of classification tasks, such as the identification of images and optical characters. However, they suffer from a serious limitation. They lack a memory for recording the output values of units in previous processing steps of the network. As a result, they were not able to reliably track relations among non-adjacent elements of an input string, where these relations span significant distances over the sequence. So, for example, they could not handle nesting and embedding in a series of parentheses, like $(_1 (_2 (_3 (_4)_4 (_5)_5)_3)_2 (_6 (_7 (_8)_8 (_9)_9)_7)_6)_1$. Each left parenthesis is closed by a corresponding right parenthesis in this string, with the higher numbers marking the more deeply nested parentheses. The lower numbers correspond to larger, less deeply nested units, defined by parentheses that are farther apart.

These long-distance relations figure in complex structures, such as grammatical relations between subjects, verbs, and objects, which can connect noun phrases (NPs) and verbs across intervening and nested phrases. An example of such a relation is the subject-verb agreement between the main plural subject NP *The candidates* and its main plural verb *give* in 1.1. This agreement runs across the singular verbs and NPs in the phrases that modify the nouns in the sentence.

1.1. *The candidates* interviewed for the position at the university where my friend teaches *give* a talk on their research

It is formally analogous to the matching of the outer most left and right parentheses, $(_1)_1$, in the sequence $(_1 (_2 (_3 (_4)_4 (_5)_5)_3)_2 (_6 (_7 (_8)_8 (_9)_9)_7)_6)_1$.

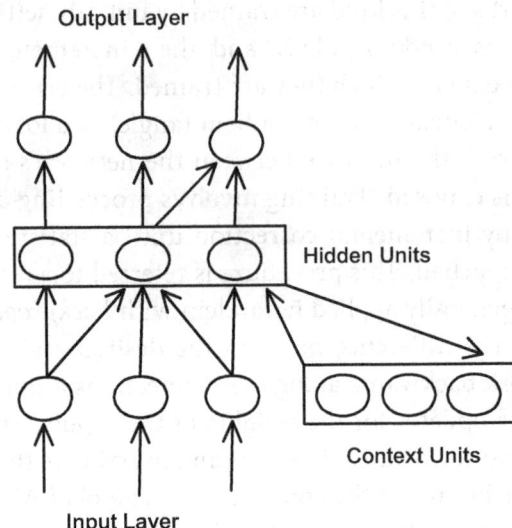

FIGURE 1.4 Simple Recurrent Network. From Clark and Lappin (2011).

Elman (1990) proposed Simple Recurrent Networks (SRNs) that contain a layer of context units which make the previous outputs of the feedforward network's hidden intermediary layers available to the hidden units in the next processing cycle. Figure 1.4 gives a schematic representation of an SRN.

Elman (1990) used an SRN to recognise syntactic relations between noun-verb and noun-verb-noun patterns. Elman (1991, 1998) applied an SRN to recognise a context-free fragment of English that contains embedded subjects and objects in relative clauses.[6]

Minsky and Papert (1969) argued that neural networks are unable to learn the rules and patterns that support complex human reasoning. They proposed that it is necessary to represent knowledge through symbolic systems and to apply rules to these representations in order to capture higher level human cognitive operations of this kind. Minsky (1991) suggested that hybrid systems, combining neural networks for lower-level perceptual classification and symbolic components for reasoning, are needed for progress in AI.[7]

1.4 SYMBOLIC RULE-BASED AI

Mathematical logic provides a formalised system for representing information and rules for deriving conclusions from assumptions.[8] Using logic for knowledge representation and inference is an important area of work in symbolic AI. Employing logic to test a system for constraint satisfaction is a central application of this kind. One way of formalising a constraint is as a conjunctive list of alternative conditions, where each condition is encoded as a propositional letter or its negation (either as A or not-A). These are known as *literals*. Such a list is a conjunction of disjunctions, and it is described as being in *conjunctive normal form* (CNF). Testing the constraint for satisfiability involves trying to find an assignment of truth values to its literals that renders the entire statement true. This is the satisfaction (SAT) problem.

Consider a simple example of constraint satisfaction formulated as a SAT problem. Imagine a small town with one railway track going through it from east to west. The track in the town is used by trains travelling between destinations beyond the town in each direction. In order to avoid collisions, the railway operator must ensure that no two trains pass through the town at the same time. This imposes a scheduling constraint on rail traffic. Let A be the statement that a train is coming through the town from the east at a specified time and date, and let B be the statement that a train is coming through the town from the west at the same time and date. Then either not-A or not-B must hold for every time and date. If one considers the problem of scheduling train routes throughout an entire country, it is clear that a large number of constraints is required to maintain the consistency, safety, and smooth running of the system.

Increasing the set of constraints that have to be tested to control complex systems may produce a combinatorial explosion. In the general case, not all SAT problems can be solved in a manageable amount of time using deterministic procedures.[9] However, there are efficient SAT constraint solvers that do provide tractable solutions to large subclasses of these problems.[10] While SAT problems and constraint solvers remain an active area of AI research, they are limited to specific issues of planning and organisation. They are not particularly useful in many other domains of AI.

Much human reasoning relies on typicality judgements to the effect that normal elements of a class of objects or events instantiate a cluster of properties. However, exceptions to these assumptions do exist. So, birds typically fly, but chickens, penguins, and ostriches don't. It is generally the case that Quakers are pacifists, and US Republicans are not. However, at least one Republican, Richard Nixon, was a Quaker, but not a pacifist. Reducing inflation frequently requires a rise in interest rates, which tends to cause unemployment. But the interest rate rise and subsequent fall in inflation in 2023–2024 was accompanied by near full employment during this period.

Default reasoning involves drawing defeasible conclusions from premisses that hold in typical situations, but which permit exceptions. It is non-monotonic in nature. If one adds new information to these premisses, it may overturn the conclusion. This happens in each of the three examples given above, where a deviation from a typicality-based inference is cited. By contrast, classical logics are monotonic, in that adding new statements to a set of premises in a valid inference preserves the entailment. Therefore, (unmodified) classical logics are not able to capture default reasoning. Developing non-monotonic systems of inference has been a major concern within symbolic, rule-based AI.

One way of implementing this project is to construct a formal non-monotonic logic designed to capture the set of entailments that default-based inference generates.[11] Interesting work has been done in this area, but there are a variety of formal and computational problems that attach to most of these logics. One of the main difficulties is sustaining the consistency of such a logic, while encoding the rich set of interacting principles required to yield the inferences and exceptions exhibited in actual cases of reasoning. A second challenge is to ensure that the logic is sufficiently expressive to capture non-monotonic inference patterns, but that it is restricted enough to allow us to effectively identify all of its relevant entailments.

Minksy (1974) proposes a network of frames, rather than a logic, for representing the structure of default reasoning. Frames are templates that are organised as attribute types and values which fill slots with default values. The templates specify typicality conditions on classes of objects and events in a structured ontological network. Subframes can fill slot values, and they inherit the attribute values of their parent frames, unless the defaults are blocked by exceptions. Table 1.1 gives a partial frame for birds, and Table 1.2 for penguins. The ISA relation indicates that the frame for penguins is a subframe for birds. The default value for Body Cover, Feathers, is inherited, but the default value for Mode of Locomotion, Fly, is not.

As in the case of a non-monotonic logic, constructing a frame network poses significant problems of sustaining consistency of attributes and values, while achieving expressive completeness and computational efficiency. Such networks quickly become complex and problematic, as attributes, slots, and values are added to frames to accommodate cases of default reasoning.

TABLE 1.1 Partial Frame for Birds.

Type	Value	Slot
This Frame	–	Bird
ISA	Animal	Parent Frame
Body Cover	Feathers	Default
Mode of Locomotion	Fly	Default

TABLE 1.2   Partial Frame for Penguins.

Type	Value	Slot
This Frame	–	Penguin
ISA	Bird	Parent Frame
Body Cover	Feathers	Default Inherited from Parent Frame
Locomotion	Walk/Swim/Slide	Default Not Inherited from Parent Frame

Scripts (Schank and Abelson, 1977) provide an alternative mechanism for knowledge representation through paradigms, that is closely related to frames. A script consists of a sequence of schematic scenes connected through actions. It represents a prototypical narrative pattern of default expectations, plans, and behaviour that surround events in the world.

Weizenbaum (1966)'s ELIZA was an early computational dialogue system that used keywords and elementary scripts to simulate a sympathetic psycho-therapist reacting to patients' typed comments. Despite the highly restricted range of the program's output and the largely canned nature of its responses, it inspired many of its users to engage seriously with it. This seems to be a reflection of a strong human tendency to attribute intelligence and intention even to simple computational devices that produce apparently relevant natural language interaction. ELIZA was one of the first chatbots. As we will see in Chapter 2, current chatbots do not employ frames or scripts, but have a very different architecture. They rely on powerful LLMs to generate complex, human-like responses to prompts, over a wide range of domains and topics.

Rule-based systems have also been used to encode grammars that parse input strings. Such grammars played an important role in representing the structure and interpretation of natural language sentences in NLP. Pereira and Warren (1980) propose Definite Clause Grammars (DCGs) as a general system for writing grammars in a logic programming framework. DCG rules are *Horn clauses*, which are disjunctions of literals that contain at most one positive (non-negated literal). This requires that they be of the form *H or not-B_1 or...or not-B_k*. A Horn clause of this type is equivalent to the re-write rule $H \leftarrow B_1, \ldots , B_k$, where H is the head of the rule, and $B_1, \ldots , B_k$ the body of conditions that must each hold in order for H to be the case. The literals are predicates with arguments that can be constants or variables. DCGs can capture long-distance dependencies, like parenthesis matching, and subject-verb number agreement.[12]

Consider a simplified case in which all left parentheses precede all right parentheses. The DCG in (1) enforces parenthesis closure for this set of strings. The head s covers the full string. [1] and [r] are single member lists of the left and right parentheses, respectively. The first rule is recursive. It calls itself through the appearance of s in the body of the rule. The implication arrow is a re-write instruction. The commas between items on the right side of the rules are conjunctions (and), indicating that all of these conditions must hold for the head to be satisfied. Every string with *n* number of 1s on the left will contain *n* rs to the right of the last 1.[13]

```
(1) s --> [1],s,[r].

    s --> [1],[r].
```

(2) is a very simple grammar for number agreement between subject NPs and main verb phrases (VPs). The ; in the third rule is *or* (a disjunction). The underscore in this rule is an anonymous variable, which can be replaced by any item satisfying the rule for np(N) (the second rule).

```
(2) s(N) --> np(N), vp(N).

    np(N) --> det(N), noun(N).

    vp(N) --> verb(N) ; verb(N), np(_).

    det(_) --> [D],
      {det_list(L), member(D,L)}.

    noun(singular) --> [A],
      {sing_noun_list(L), member(A,L)}.

    noun(plural) --> [B],
      {plural_noun_list(L), member(B,L)}.

    verb(singular) --> [V],
      {sing_verb_list(L), member(V,L)}.

    verb(plural) --> [V],
      {plural_verb_list(L), member(V,L)}.

    det_list([the,some]).

    sing_noun_list([boy,house]).

    plural_noun_list([boys,houses]).

    sing_verb_list([likes,paints]).

    plural_verb_list([like,paint]).
```

The variable N carries the value of grammatical number, which comes from lexical lists at the end of the grammar, and it is passed up through noun, np, verb, and vp predicates. The first rule of the grammar ensures that the number of the subject NP and that of the VP are identical. It has to match the N value in both. This grammar will generate sentences like *The boys paint the house*, but it will block *The boy like the house*.

In addition to cases like these, DCGs can capture complex cross-serial dependencies of the form $a^n b^m c^n d^m$, which are exemplified by syntactic structures in languages like Swiss German.

These structures take natural languages into the class of mildly context-sensitive languages (Shieber, 1985; Joshi et al., 1990).

A variety of computational grammar formalisms have been developed to implement alternative views of the syntax and the semantics of natural language sentences.[14] A dependency grammar (Nivre, 2006) represents the syntactic relations of a phrase as directed dependencies between terms of different types and the head of the phrase that they attach to. The main verb serves as the head of the entire sentence. This framework provides a representation of the hierarchical syntactic structure of a sentence that maps transparently into semantic predicate-argument and predicate-modifier patterns. It has been influential in parsing and semantic interpretation. Figure 1.5 gives a labelled dependency parse graph for the sentence *This time around, they're moving even faster.*

1.5 PROBABILISTIC METHODS

Probability theory has many of the advantages of the non-monotonic systems considered in Section 1.4, but it avoids several of their difficulties. It captures defeasible inferences through probability models. These assign precise quantitative values to the joint likelihood of a set of events represented in the model, where some of these are conditioned by others. When new

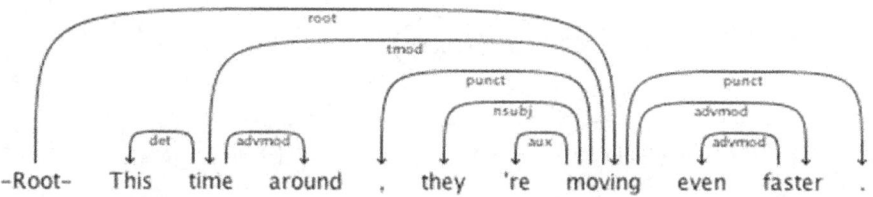

FIGURE 1.5   Labelled dependency parse. From the Stanford Natural Language Processing Group, https://nlp.stanford.edu/software/nndep.html.

information is introduced, these values are updated through the principles of the probability theory.[15] It is not necessary to introduce distinct rules of inference, frames, or scripts for each new case that arises. Probability theory is a logic constructed to reason about uncertainty and to reflect agents' beliefs about the likelihood of alternative states of affairs. It is designed to accommodate the revision of belief through the dynamic update of information, which produces a re-computation of probabilities throughout the system.

Bayesian networks have been influential in modelling inference and belief in AI.[16] They are (acyclic directed) graphs with *random variables* at their nodes. Each random variable encodes a set of possible events or states, where each element of this set is assigned a probability value. The arrows specify dependency relations that correspond to conditional probabilities. These are local. A node in the graph depends only on its parent node, and not on nodes higher than its parent.

Figure 1.6 is an example of a simple Bayesian network in which each node is a random variable with a Boolean state, True or False. The likelihood that one of these states holds is specified by a probability value, which is conditional on the state of its parent node. As Cloudy has no parent, its likelihood (the weather is cloudy or it is not) is not conditioned. Whether the Sprinkler is on or off, and whether it is raining or dry depends on the value of the Cloudy variable. The likelihood of the grass being wet is conditioned by the values of Sprinkler and Rain. If all these values are known, then the model specifies a complete *joint probability distribution* (JPD) for the events that it represents. The probability that the grass is wet is the sum of the joint probabilities of the grass being wet, the sprinkler being on, rain coming down, and the weather being cloudy.

As the number of nodes and arcs in a Bayesian network expands, the complexity of computing its JPD increases sharply, and it quickly becomes intractable. However, there are sampling and estimation procedures that permit the JPDs for a large class of networks to be efficiently determined.[17]

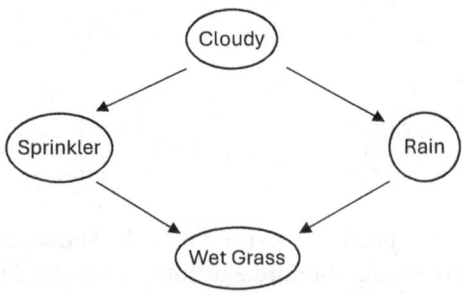

FIGURE 1.6   Bayesian network. Based on Norvig and Russell (2020).

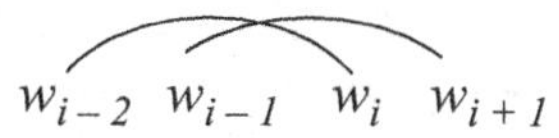

$$w_{i-2} \quad w_{i-1} \quad w_i \quad w_{i+1}$$

FIGURE 1.7   Lexical trigram.

Markov models are another Bayesian probability method that has been widely used in AI, particularly in NLP. They predict the next item w_i in a sequence s on the basis of the previous n elements of s. These are N-gram models, which predict the ith item in a chain on the basis of its $i - n$ items. In a bigram model, the probability if w_i depends on the immediately preceding element w_{i-1}, in a trigram model on the preceding two items, etc. Figure 1.7 shows the dependency pattern of a trigram model. If we take w to be a word, then it is a lexical trigram model for predicting words in a string.

When an N-gram is limited to a small number, as in the case of a bigram model, the N-grams will tend to occur with higher frequency in the data set (corpus) on which the model is trained. However, long-distance dependencies cannot be captured by short N-grams. Conversely, longer N-grams capture more non-adjacent dependency relations, but they are less frequent in the data.

Bayesian Hidden Markov Models (HMMs) predict the occurrence of unseen items or events on the basis of observed events, and beliefs concerning the prior likelihood of the observed events, using Bayes theorem.[18] The formula for Bayes theorem is $p(e \mid u) = p(u \mid e)p(e) / p(u)$, where e is the observed event, and u is the unobserved event. This theorem states that the conditional probability of an observed event e, given an unobserved event u, is the product of the probability of u given e (as predicted by the model) and the prior probability of e (an updated probability specified by the model), divided by the unconditional probability of u. HMMs apply this principle to a training set in which both instances of e and of u occur to extract predictions for the next u, given preceding cases of e and u in a sequence.

Let w be a word, and c an unseen word class. Figure 1.8 shows a second-order HMM for words and word classes, where the word and the class that it belongs to depend on the previous two word classes.

Statistical methods of this kind were particularly influential in speech recognition (Jelinek, 1998) and machine translation (Brown et al., 1990). The problem of speech recognition can be specified as predicting the (unseen) word that corresponds to a set of observed phonetic features. If we formulate it in terms of an HMM, this involves identifying the most probable word, given a set of sounds. It is possible to describe the task of machine translation as generating the words of a target language sentence from

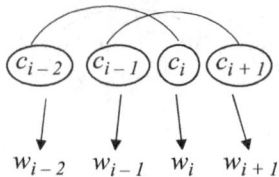

FIGURE 1.8   Second-order HMM for word classes.

those of a source language sentence, when our probability model has been trained on a corpus of aligned sentence pairs from each of these languages.

Chomsky (1957) claimed that statistical methods are irrelevant to characterising grammaticality, because a simple bigram model cannot distinguish between 1.2(a) and 1.2(b).

1.2 (a) Colourless green ideas sleep furiously.
     (b) Furiously sleep ideas green colourless.

It assigns both strings nil probability, given that neither appeared in spoken or written data, at the time that Chomsky's book was first published. 1.2(a) is syntactically well formed, but semantically anomalous, while 1.2(b) is ungrammatical. This argument has been widely accepted among theoretical linguists over many years. However, it is unsound. Pereira (2000) demonstrated that a bigram model, with smoothing (a technique used to assign non-null probabilities to unseen events and word classes), gives significantly higher probability to 1.2(a) than to 1.2(b), when it has been trained on a corpus of newspaper text.[19]

In fact, an earlier method for assigning non-null probability to unseen events, the Good-Turing smoothing procedure, was published in 1953 (Good, 1953). Therefore, it was possible to recognise Chomsky's (1957) argument for the impossibility of characterising grammaticality in terms of probability, as formally unsound at the time that it first appeared. It was already known then among statisticians that events with no frequency did not necessarily receive nil probability. However, Chomsky's argument continued to enjoy wide acceptance among theoretical linguists until recently. This would seem to be a particularly clear case of the unfortunate confusions which can arise when theorists make strong claims about phenomena treated in a particular discipline (in this case, probability theory), while ignoring relevant technical results in that field. I will return to Good-Turing smoothing, and the general problem of estimating the likelihood of unseen events, in Chapter 4, in discussing the issue of superintelligent agents.

Statistical methods are frequently combined with the symbolic systems discussed in Section 1.4. So, for example, the rules of a grammar may have probabilities attached to them to yield a probabilistic grammar. These are learned from the frequency of parse structures in a training corpus annotated with the analyses that the grammar generates. The rules of a non-monotonic logic can be assigned probability values, as can frames and scripts, to condition their activation on certain contexts. Also, feedforward neural networks, described in Section 1.3, generate probability distributions over possible outputs to rank them for likelihood. Probability models are, then, pervasive across a wide variety of AI systems.

One of the main differences between symbolic AI systems on one side and statistical models and neural networks on the other is that the latter incorporate learning procedures as part of their design, but rules and templates do not. Probability models and neural networks are trained on data, through learning algorithms, to extract the generalisations that they apply to new cases. Machine learning is the area of AI that studies efficient and reliable procedures for acquiring predictive models from data sets. It is possible to use machine learning techniques to infer certain symbolic rule-based systems, but these are external to the systems themselves.[20]

1.6 THE SEASONS OF AI

From the genesis of AI, a cyclic pattern emerged of an initial heady optimism concerning the potential of AI research to produce broad coverage intelligent software and robotic systems, followed by widespread disappointment in the progress actually achieved. The optimism was frequently accompanied by wildly unrealistic expectations of what the current models could do. The first instance of this cycle saw an AI spring, with a flourishing of work on neural networks and on various approaches to machine translation during the 1950s through the 1960s. By the end of the latter decade, it had become clear that the products of this work suffered from serious limitations of accuracy, scale, and efficiency.

A number of influential reports and publications contributed to the growing scepticism that had started to set in. Bar-Hillel (1960) argued that fully automatic machine translation was an unrealistic objective. Accurate translation requires knowledge of the influence of both linguistic and pragmatic context on interpretation of lexical items and phrases. Bar-Hillel asserted that it is not clear how this sort of information, and the principles for applying it, can be effectively encoded in computational models. He suggested that machine-assisted translation, where the output of a machine translation program is subject to human editing and correction, is a more reasonable approach. The Automatic Language Processing Advisory Committee (ALPAC, 1966) published a report for the US National Academy of Sciences and the National Research Council, which expressed similar doubts on the prospects for accurate, large-scale machine translation programs.[21]

Minksy and Papert's (1969) critique of neural networks, briefly described in Section 1.3, intensified doubts on the possibility of capturing central cognitive capacities within this framework. In the United Kingdom, the Science Research Council commissioned James Lighthill, a professor of applied mathematics at Cambridge University, to write a report on the state of AI (Lighthill, 1973). He considered the likelihood that the AI research being conducted in Britain at the time would create useful engineering products, or that it would make significant contributions to basic science. His conclusions reflected the general scepticism that had taken root in large parts of the scientific and engineering communities.

As a result of this environment, an AI winter set in, where the discipline experienced significant cuts in public funding and reductions in commercial investment. Minksy's critique promoted a turn towards rule-based non-monotonic reasoning and other symbolic methods, which were prominent throughout the 1970s and 1980s. By the end of the 1980s, it had become clear that small-scale symbolic models could not be easily scaled up into comprehensive working systems. Rules, templates, and features needed to be coded, and exceptions had to be accommodated by hand-crafted conditions. The process of developing such programs is enormously labour intensive, and to support them over time requires very substantial resources. The systems are brittle. They break when they encounter cases not covered by their rule or feature sets. Once again, widespread doubts about the viability of AI, this time in its symbolic mode, set in.

The late 1980s saw renewed interest in neural networks, with the emergence of more effective procedures for training them and alternative architectures for implementing them.[22] The limitations of the hardware on which these systems were running were an important factor in constraining their success in the initial phases of their development. The first generation of computers built in the late 1940s and throughout the 1950s used vacuum tubes for processing and magnetic tape for storing data. Programs were written and run on cards.

Transistors and integrated circuits replaced vacuum tubes in the 1960s. The rise of microchip processors and hard drives in the 1970s produced a significant expansion in processing power, memory, and storage, together with a substantial reduction in the size of computing equipment. Programming could be done electronically and interactively on screens. Workstations and personal computers began to replace large mainframes.

However, it was not until the commercial development of *graphics processing units* (GPUs) in the late 1990s that it was possible to use massively parallel regimens to train neural networks on large amounts of data, in comparatively short periods of time. This engineering advance facilitated the development and testing of large, architecturally complex neural networks in ways that were not possible on previous generations of computers with more limited processing and storage capacities.

Statistical methods also gained increasing acceptance in the late 1980s, particularly in NLP. The models that these methods generate had previously been restricted in coverage and accuracy by the absence of large amounts of data in electronically accessible form. As the quantity of digital resources increased, these models became easier to train and test over different applications. So, for example, Brown et al. (1990) used the machine-readable version of Hansard, the bilingual proceedings of the Canadian Parliament, as a source of 3 million pairs of aligned English-French sentence pairs to train their statistical machine translation system. The expansion of digital resources in different languages, visual images, and sound (including speech) was also an important element in the improvement in training neural networks over a variety of tasks. In Chapter 2, I will consider how these developments, together with major design changes in neural networks, generated the revolution in AI systems that has emerged over the past 15 years.

NOTES

1 https://aiindex.stanford.edu/wp-content/uploads/2023/04/HAI_ AI-Index-Report_2023.pdf.

2 See Shieber (2004) for a variety of views on the Turing test.

3 See Norvig and Russell (2020) for a comprehensive introduction to the methods and approaches that have been influential in AI.

4 I am grateful to Haim Dubossarsky for helpful suggestions on how to present perceptrons and neural networks.

5 Rumelhart et al. (1986a) introduced backpropagation. For the early history of neural networks and connectionism, see Eberhart and Dobbins (1990), and Widrow and Lehrer (1990).

6 Clark and Lappin (2011) discuss multilayer feedforward networks and SRNs in NLP.

7 This view has also been advanced concerning current Deep Neural Networks. See, for example, Marcus (2022). Lappin (2021, 2024) considers various attempts to integrate symbolic grammars into DNNs, and he argues that they have not, as yet, shown significant improvements in performance. Lappin (2025) considers two alternative architectures for neuro-symbolic models. One injects symbolic content directly into the layers of a DNN. The second feeds the output of a DNN to a rule-based reasoning system in a federative framework.

The injective approach has not, to date, yielded significant improvements in performance relative to the corresponding non-hybrid DNN. By contrast, the federative architecture has achieved some interesting and hopeful results. It seems closer to Minksky's original suggestion. More research on both architectures is needed to explore their possibilities and their limitations.

8 Mendelsohn (2015) gives a comprehensive introduction to classical propositional and first-order logic, with a discussion of completeness and decidability results. It includes chapters on computability and Turing machines, and on set theory, as well as appendices on modal and second-order logic.

9 The class of SAT problems is NP complete. See Papadimitriou (1995) for computational complexity and NP completeness.

10 See Mackworth (1992), Tamura et al. (2010), and Bofill et al. (2012) for discussions of SAT solvers.

11 Reiter (1987) gives a detailed overview of non-monotonic logics, as well as a summary of non-logical frameworks for expressing default reasoning. Fuzzy logic and fuzzy set theory (Zadeh, 1965, 1975) are related alternative systems for paradigm-driven reasoning.

12 Pereira and Warren (1980) show that DCGs are at least as powerful and efficient as Woods' (1970) Augmented Transition Networks for parsing and natural language analysis. They can encode Context-Sensitive Grammars.

13 This is a set of $a^n b^n$ strings, which is a context-free language.

14 See Lappin (2021), Chapter 6, for a brief discussion of alternative grammar formalisms in NLP.

15 See Halpern (2003) for a clear and comprehensive introduction to probability theory, and its applications in AI.

16 Pearl and Russell (2003) provide a brief introduction to Bayesian networks. Lappin (2018) proposes that Bayesian networks be used for natural language semantics. Bernardy et al. (2022) develop a compositional Bayesian inference semantics for natural language.

17 Computing the JPD for the elements of the full class of Bayesian networks is, in general, NP hard. See Pearl and Russell (2003), and Lappin (2018) for discussion of methods that can render the task tractable for a significant subclass of networks.

18 See Fosler-Lussier (1998), Lau et al. (2017), and Jurafsky and Martin (2023) for Markov models, N-gram models, and HMMs in NLP. Manning and Schütze (1999) provide an introduction to statistical methods in NLP.

19 Lau et al. (2017) characterise sentence acceptability in terms of probability, but they argue that grammaticality cannot be reduced to probability for formal reasons. They use machine learning models to predict human sentence acceptability judgements. Lau et al. (2020) apply transformers and LLMs to predict acceptability judgements in document context.

20 Lappin and Shieber (2007), and Clark and Lappin (2011) explore the application of machine learning (computational learning theory) to the task of grammar induction.

21 See Poibeau (2017) on the impact of the ALPAC report on machine translation, and AI generally.

22 Rumelhart et al. (1986b) marked an important point in the return of neural networks to the forefront of AI research.

CHAPTER 2

The Deep Learning Revolution

2.1 HARDWARE INNOVATION AND THE EXPANSION OF DIGITAL DATA

The Hungarian American mathematician John von Neumann developed the architecture that has dominated digital computing since its inception in the 1940s. It contains a central processor that performs the operations which implement the instructions of a program, and a memory unit for storing both the program and the data to which the operations are applied. The information contained in the program and the data flow through a common connection (a bus) to the processor, and the results of its operations are sent back through this connection to the memory store. As the complexity of the program and the amount of data increase, traffic through the bus becomes clogged with information units, creating what is known as *von Neumann's bottleneck*. The result of the bottleneck is that a processor handles program instructions and data faster than they can be accessed from memory. The processor stands idle for increasing amounts of time, as it waits for new instructions and data input.

Intel introduced the first microchip central processing unit (CPU), its 4004, in 1971. As CPU microchips became increasingly powerful, with additional processing cores, memory expanded, and the speed of random access memory (RAM) increased, the possibility of handling large quantities of data more efficiently improved. The bottleneck problem remained,

DOI: 10.1201/9781003624790-2

but processing time was greatly reduced. Using clusters of CPUs produced powerful computing systems, but these continued to process data in a largely sequential pipeline, by virtue of the design of CPUs.

In 1999, Nvidia released the first graphics processing unit (GPU) processor, the GeForce 256. Unlike CPUs, GPUs consist of multiple processing units that perform a large number of operations in tandem. Their highly parallelised architecture allows them to multiply matrices of vectors much more quickly than CPUs. They were originally created to handle the massive amount of parallel processing required to sustain effective graphics for computer gaming. It was soon recognised that they are particularly well suited to processing the large data needed to train neural networks. They are orders of magnitude faster in performing these computations than CPUs, even when the latter are organised into clusters. As GPUs increased in power, they have been able to substantially reduce the time required to train large deep neural networks (DNNs) on big data sets. Their development has been a major force in driving the deep learning revolution.

Google deployed its first tensor processing unit (TPU) in 2015, and it made TPUs available for general use through cloud computing in 2018. While CPUs and GPUs are general-purpose processors, TPUs are designed for specific applications in machine learning. They surpass GPUs in speed and processing power for a range of matrix operations that are required for DNN training and applications.[1]

Quantum computing has become increasingly influential as an alternative to conventional computing architecture. Classical binary computers represent information through bits that are in one of two states, 1 or 0. Quantum computers employ qubits, in which 1 and 0 states are combined through superposition in a state that constitutes a probability of being 1, together with a probability of being 0. This state represents a probability amplitude. Qubits interfere with each other. They can also be entangled with each other at an unbounded distance. These are properties inherent in the physics of quantum mechanics. Collections of qubits encode exponentially more information than corresponding sets of bits. As a result, a quantum circuit can compute results exponentially faster than a conventional binary computing system. Therefore, in principle, a quantum computer can process data and apply algorithms far more quickly and efficiently than binary computers.[2]

In fact, qubits are highly unstable in that they are susceptible to interference and disruption from entanglement with external elements of the environment. This causes *decoherence*, which produces errors and unreliability in quantum computations. Current quantum computing systems are in their infancy, with limited computational capacity. They have to be cooled at near absolute zero temperatures. Numerous hardware issues remain before they can be developed into efficient large-scale computing systems. The largest current quantum computers, like IBM's Condor, have slightly more than 1,100 qubits.

Two of the most important formal results which demonstrate that quantum computing is, in principle, faster than conventional binary processing are Shor's algorithm for identifying the prime factors of an integer and Grover's algorithm for unstructured search. The former is useful for cryptography. The latter may well yield important savings in time and complexity for machine learning applications using large amounts of data, but these are some way off in the future. Before such applications can be run on quantum circuits, it will be necessary to achieve significant improvements in the robustness and reliability of the hardware that realises these circuits.

In the early years of AI machine-readable text and other sorts of digital data were close to non-existent. The information required to train neural networks and statistical models had to be handcrafted for each task. This greatly constrained the possibilities for implemented work on machine learning. With the emergence of digital records and the rise of the internet, the situation changed drastically, within a comparatively short period of time. Automatic data gathering from repositories like *Wikipedia* and social media yielded a wealth of digital content in a variety of modalities, including natural language text, graphic images, and sounds. As internet use spread throughout much of the world, with laptops and smartphones becoming common accessories, the range and diversity of this data also expanded dramatically. Crowd source platforms like Amazon Mechanical Turk made it possible to solicit machine-readable human responses for virtually any experimental task at speeds and costs that had not been possible in the past.

With vastly increased processing power, DNNs could be trained on large amounts of data in manageable periods of time. As the stream of digital content became a flood, machine learning began to flourish in the era of big data. Innovation in processing hardware and digitalisation of data provided the infrastructure for the progress of recent years in AI. But the actual revolution turned on radical innovations in the design of neural networks. These have come in what we can identify as two successive waves of change.

2.2 THE FIRST WAVE: RECURRENT AND CONVOLUTIONAL NEURAL NETWORKS

In Chapter 1, I discussed feedforward neural networks and Elman's (1990) Recurrent Neural Networks (RNNs). The latter is a sequential processing system with a memory. Both types of networks apply functions to input data encoded as vectors of a fixed size to yield output vectors of specified length. RNNs generate a sequence of output vectors. They preserve information obtained from previous processing steps for the string. The structure of an RNN is shown in Figure 2.1.

Simple RNNs do not filter or control the information passed between earlier and later states. As a result, they are not able to reliably recognise the variety of long-distance dependency relations that hold among disparate elements of their input data.

An additional problem with RNNs, and with deep feedforward neural networks, is that when backpropagation is used to compute the gradient of the loss function in training, this gradient can become vanishingly small, or it can explode into unmanageably large values.[3] The vanishing gradient problem arises when the derivative of the gradient at each time step of the RNN, or at each hidden layer of the feedforward network, is small. As these values are multiplied backwards through the network in successive pairs of layers, they continue to decrease until they approach 0.

Exploding gradients are caused when successive derivatives are large, and backward computation of the loss function causes them to expand from the output to the input layer of the network. In the first case, the error signal is lost, while in the second case, the error function cannot converge on corrected weights. Learning fails with both types of perverse gradient pattern.

There are various ways of fixing these problems. So, for example, vanishing gradients can be avoided by normalising all gradient derivatives in a network to avoid extreme values. It is possible to exclude exploding

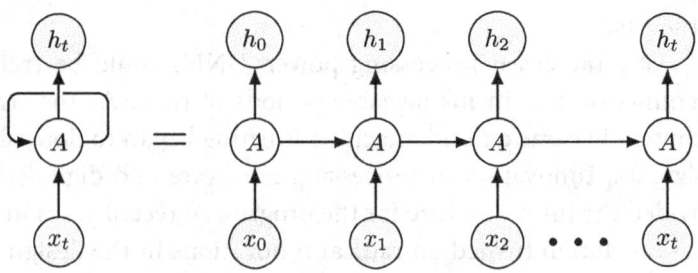

FIGURE 2.1   Recurrent Neural Network. From Lappin (2021).

gradients by imposing constraints on the size of gradient derivatives as they increase through backpropagation. As we will see in Section 2.4, neither of these problems arise with transformers.

To solve the recognition of long-distance dependencies, Hochreiter and Schmidhuber (1997) introduced a type of RNN known as the Long Short-Term Memory (LSTM) network. Each of its processing units applies three functions to its input vectors, where these functions act as filtering gates that determine which information is passed on to the next processing phase. The forgetting gate identifies that part of the input which is discarded. The input gate updates the remaining part of the vector with content from a new constituent of the input vector. The output gate produces the vector that is transmitted to the next processing unit of the network. Figure 2.2 gives the architecture of an LSTM.[4]

Cho et al. (2014) propose the Gated Recurrent Unit (GRU) as an alternative RNN model which also filters input vectors in each processing unit of the sequence. It has only an update and a reset gate, and so it performs filtering and processing with a simpler architecture than an LSTM. Both LSTMs and GRUs avoid vanishing gradients by applying activation functions like ReLU (rectified linear unit), which prevent sequences of derivative values for a gradient from disappearing over the length of a network.

LSTMs and GRUs have achieved considerable success in a variety of NLP (natural language processing) applications. Linzen et al. (2016) show that an LSTM trained on Wikipedia text obtains high accuracy in learning subject-verb matching in English, even when the subject is separated from its verb by an increasingly large set of intervening NPs (noun phrases) with grammatical number different than the subject, as in 2.1(a)–(d).

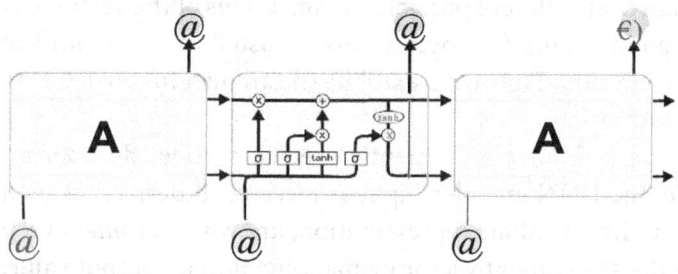

FIGURE 2.2 Long Short-Term Memory. From Christopher Olah's blog *Understanding LSTM Networks*, August 7, 2015.

2.1

(a) *The students submit* a final project to complete the course.

(b) *The students* enrolled in the program *submit* a final project to complete the course.

(c) *The students* enrolled in the program in the Department *submit* a final project to complete the course.

(d) *The students* enrolled in the program in the Department where my colleague teaches *submit* a final project to complete the course.

Bernardy and Lappin (2017) confirm Linzen et al.'s results, and they extend them to cases with greater numbers of intervening NPs. They test both LSTMs and GRUs under various configurations and parameter values. They find that their levels of performance for the agreement task are comparable.

Gulordava et al. (2018) use an LSTM to achieve highly accurate recognition of subject-verb agreement across several languages. They also provide evidence that the LSTM is able to discern hierarchical syntactic structure, and that it approaches human levels of performance for the different language data sets that they test their model on.

Convolutional Neural Networks (CNNs; LeCun et al., 2010) have a different architecture than RNNs. A convolutional layer identifies a feature map from input data by recognising subcomponents of this data. A pooling layer then reduces the dimensions of the features to produce a compressed map and to render it stable under small variations. Successive convolutional and pooling layers produce increasingly high-level representations of the objects in the data. The final map is passed to fully connected layers, which turn it into a vector. A softmax function generates a probability distribution over different possible classifications of the vector. CNNs have achieved good results for applications in visual image identification and speech recognition. Figure 2.3 exhibits the architecture of a CNN used for image classification.

LSTMs and CNNs are frequently used as encoder-decoder models. In this mode, the DNN encodes input as a vector. It derives, as its final hidden state, an intermediate representation, known as a *context vector*, and it then decodes the context vector by mapping it to an output value. Models of this kind are trained on direct pairings of input and output data. From these pairings, the system learns to generate appropriate output from the

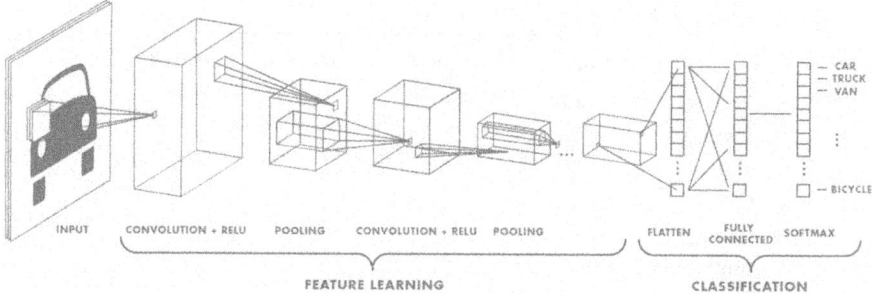

FIGURE 2.3   Convolutional Neural Network. From Sumit Saha, "A Comprehensive Guide to Convolutional Networks-the ELI5 Way", *Towards Data Science*, December 18, 2015.

Source: Reproduced in Lappin (2021).

corresponding input through incrementally adjusting the weights on the hidden layers that perform the encoding, context representation, and decoding roles. Therefore, they operate as a sequence-to-sequence (seq2seq) processing model. Encoder-decoder systems are used for machine translation, object classification, image description, and a large variety of other applications.

DNNs of different types can be combined in a single processing system. So, for example, Bizzoni and Lappin (2018) construct a DNN for identifying paraphrases of metaphorical sentences that consists of a CNN which feeds an LSTM. A metaphorical sentence and a paraphrase candidate are each given to a CNN that reduces the dimensions of its vectors. The new vector is passed to an LSTM to identify the main features of the sentence. Fully connected layers combine the metaphorical and literal sentences into a single vector. The vectors from a set of metaphor-paraphrase pairs, where the metaphor is the same in each pair, are ranked for probability. The most likely pair corresponds to the most highly valued paraphrase of the metaphorical sentence.

2.3 EMBEDDINGS

Much of the power of DNNs resides in the vector representations of the data on which they are trained. These representations, known as *embeddings*, express a variety of distributional relations among elements of this data. In the case of words, they provide a conceptual map of the co-occurrence patterns of the terms extracted from the training data. These patterns encode semantic and syntactic relations among the expressions of the corpora.

TABLE 2.1   Word Context Matrix.

	Context 1	Context 2	Context 3	Context 4
Process	25	0	14	0
Invest	0	27	3	15
Storage	14	0	22	6
Chip	13	2	16	18
Rhyme	0	32	6	7
Intonation	1	36	4	3
Generate	10	6	19	20
Parallel	27	0	17	10

Vector Space Models (VSMs) of lexical meaning are built from word context matrices specifying the frequency of words from a vocabulary in a set of contexts, as shown in Table 2.1.[5]

The rows of numbers for a word in this matrix give the (in this case, contrived) frequency with which it occurs in each context. The contexts can be documents or other words with which the word co-occurs. The vectors are lists of these numbers, and words with similar vectors exhibit related distribution patterns. So, for example, the vectors for *rhyme* [0 32 6 7] and *intonation* [1 36 4 3] are similar in their context frequency values, while those for *rhyme* and *process* [25 0 14 0] are relatively far apart.

The contexts of the matrix provide the dimensions of the vectors, and they specify the space within which the vectors are defined. It is possible to represent the vectors as lines in this space, which start from a common point. We can assess their degree of similarity by determining the angle between them. The smaller this angle is, the more similar they are. We can measure this relation with the *cosine* function, which is defined relative to the inner (dot) product of the corresponding elements in vector pairs. The formula for computing the cosine distance between two vectors is

For $v = [v_1 \ldots v_k]$, $w = [w_1 \ldots w_k]$, $cos(v,w) = \sum_{i=1}^{n} v_i w_i / \sqrt{(\sum_{i=1}^{n} v_i^2)} \cdot \sqrt{(\sum_{i=1}^{n} w_i^2)}$.

VSMs of word distribution in a corpus have a very large number of dimensions and sparse vectors with many empty context values for most words. Assume that the vocabulary that we are modelling has 50,000 words, and the contexts are the words of the vocabulary. Each vector of the VSM will have 50,000 dimensions (one for each word), and most will be empty or have very low values. The majority of words do not co-occur with any frequency, even in very large corpora. Therefore, these are not efficient representations of word distribution patterns for training data.

More compact and efficient systems for extracting and representing word distribution patterns have been devised for DNNs over the past decade. One of the first of these is Mikolov et al.'s (2013) Word2vec, which provides a procedure for extracting dense word vectors with compressed dimensions from a training corpus. It involves maximising the probability of those words with which a word is likely to appear close to within a defined left and right window of text, while minimising the probability of words with which it is not likely to occur in such a window. This is a *skip gram* model. A DNN learns it from a corpus by initially assigning arbitrary vectors to all words in the vocabulary, and then incrementally adjusting their weighted values through gradient descent. The objective of the learning algorithm is to maximise the probability of each pair of target and context words that are possible near neighbours, given the distribution patterns of the training set, and to minimise the probability of each pair that is not.[6] GloVe (Pennington et al., 2014) uses the non-zero elements in a word-word co-occurrence matrix for the training set.

BERT (Devlin et al., 2019) applies a dynamic bidirectional training regime in which words are learned for textual contexts. Learning is achieved through masking the site where the likelihood of the word is predicted. A word is assigned a distinct vector for each context in which it appears. Both the left and right contexts are visible for learning and prediction. I will return to BERT in Section 2.4.

DNNs are pre-trained with embeddings on large training corpora. It is important to note that embeddings are not restricted to text. Pixels for graphic images and sound patterns are also encoded through vector representations. Recently, large multimodal embeddings have been extracted from data to represent the distributional patterns of text in visual and sound contexts. Multimodal embeddings greatly expand the power and range of DNNs by permitting them to track relations between linguistic expressions and non-linguistic environments. This has significantly enhanced the information processing capacity of current deep learning systems.

2.4 ATTENTION

The first encoder-decoder systems generated a fixed global context vector from the final hidden state of the encoder. This provides a static representation of the input sequence in which only the final state of the encoder is visible to the decoder. Much of the information associated with earlier processing of tokens in the input is not directly accessible.

Bahdanau et al. (2015) revise this architecture to include an attention layer. This layer produces a dynamic context vector that is updated with each new token of the input sequence. The vector effectively preserves the information of each encoder hidden state. It assigns different weights to these states on the basis of their relations to the output that the decoder produces. In this way, the attentional context vector learns to align the weights of the encoded input with the elements of the decoder output. This permits the system to predict output with significantly greater accuracy than pre-attention models. Figure 2.4 exhibits an attention layer between a bidirectional RNN encoder and a left-to-right decoder.

Attention has played a major role in improving the performance of seq2seq models, such as those used in machine translation. Figure 2.5 is an attention matrix for an input and output sentence pair aligned by such an MT (machine translation) system. The number and shading of the squares along the diagonal line of the matrix indicate the degree of attention assigned to each of the pairs of elements.

2.5 THE SECOND WAVE: TRANSFORMERS

Vaswani et al. (2017) introduce transformers. These are encoder-decoder DNNs that consist entirely of blocks of multi-head attention units, connected by normalisation and feedforward layers. The general architecture of a transformer is shown in Figure 2.6.

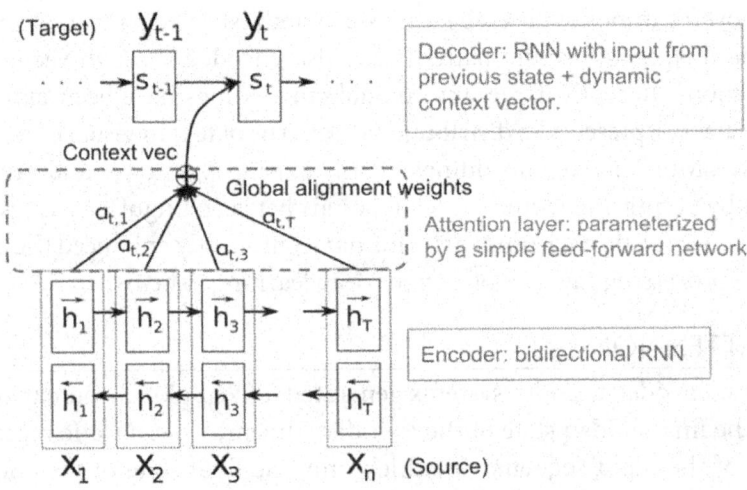

FIGURE 2.4   Encoder-decoder with attention layer. From Bahdanau et al. (2015).

Source: Reproduced in Lappin (2021).

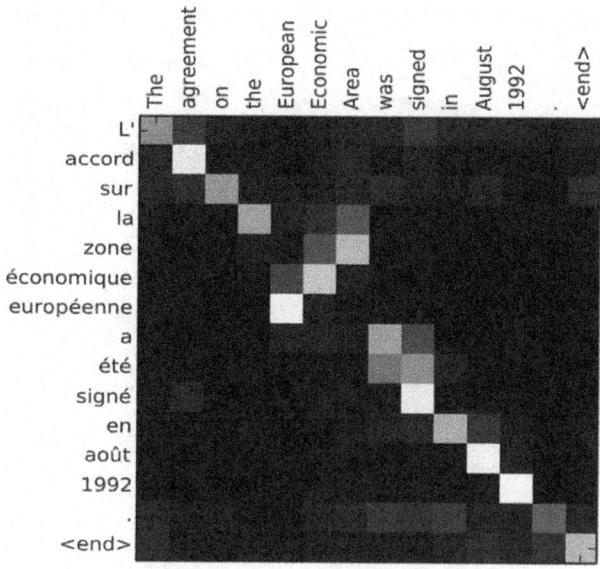

FIGURE 2.5   Attention matrix for machine translation. From Bahdanau et al. (2015).

Source: Reproduced in Lappin (2021).

Each attention block computes self-attention weights for the token of an input sequence, where self-attention is the relative importance of each token in relation to the others. The self-attention weights that a multi-head attention block assigns to the elements of an input is computed from three weight matrices consisting of the key, query, and value matrices. These weights are combined into a single vector for each token, which is passed to the normalisation and then to the feedforward layers. These layers transform each position into an output vector, which is also normalised.

While the self-attention blocks compute the weights of each token of an input sequence in relation to the others, the feedforward layers map a token's vector into an output independently of the others. The attention heads of a transformer consider all tokens simultaneously, rather than in sequence, updating their distribution of weights as they receive each token of the input. The position of each token in the sequence is encoded as separate information from the embedding vector. The encoder component of the transformer passes the normalised weight vectors to the decoder, which produces a weighted output vector. After self-attention weighting, normalisation, and feed forward layers, it applies a softmax function to the tokens of the output to obtain a probability distribution over its elements.[7]

Unidirectional transformers, like the generative models used in ChatGPT-4 from OpenAI, have masked decoders that do not see past the

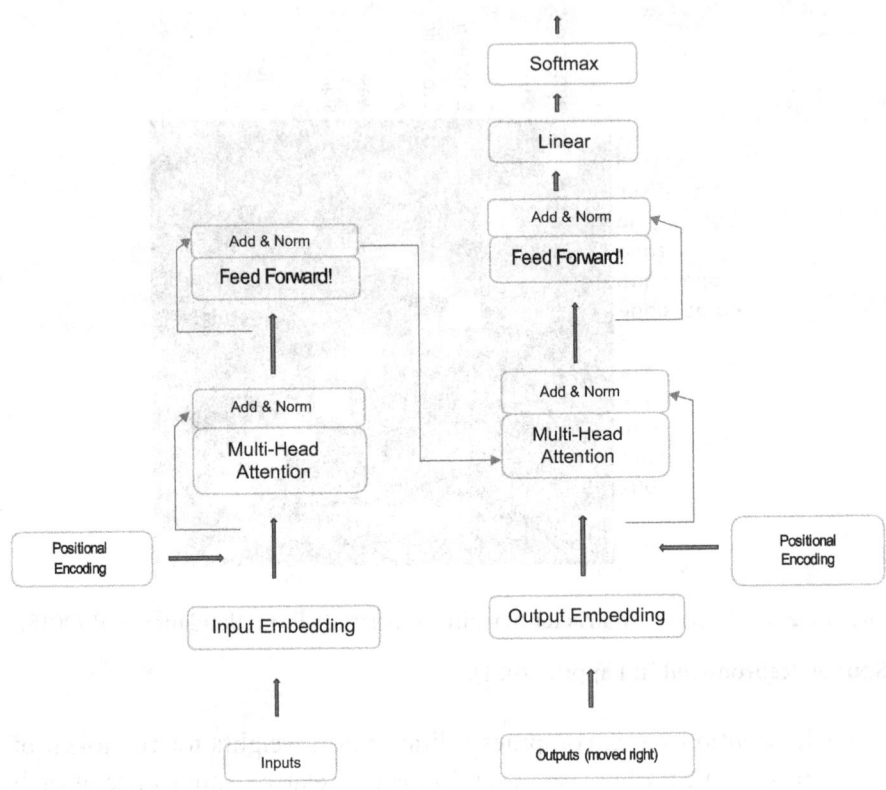

FIGURE 2.6 Architecture of a transformer. From Lappin (2021), based on Vaswani et al. (2017).

current token. They predict the next token on the basis of the conditional probabilities of possible items, given the decoded sequence of elements up to the point in the sequence that the transformer has decoded.[8]

By contrast, a bidirectional transformer like BERT (Devlin et al., 2019) is trained to predict items from both left and right contexts, by masking tokens in such contexts in the training data. Unlike unidirectional models, it can look ahead beyond the current input token, as well as at previous ones. Figure 2.7 illustrates BERT's training regime.

Each block of multi-head self-attention units in a transformer can be dedicated to a different dimension of information concerning its input. In this way, transformers can identify patterns and connections among the elements of the data on which it is pre-trained, across a wide range of features. As a result, transformers are generally more successful that LSTMs, GRU, and CNNs at recognising long-distance relations among elements in

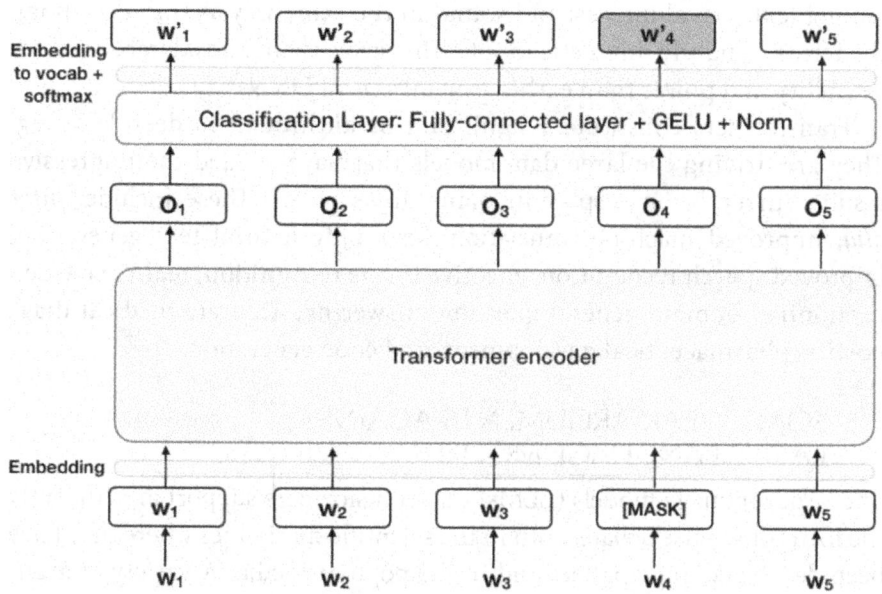

FIGURE 2.7   BERT's training regime. From Horev (2018).

Source: Reproduced in Lappin (2021).

input. They achieve higher performance on a variety of applications that require the identification of subtle and complex patterns in data.

Transformers are pre-trained on large data sets from which they extract embeddings. They can then be fine-tuned for specific applications. This involves adding new dedicated layers of attention heads or retraining some of its pre-trained layers. Data sets from a specific domain are used to train these new (or retrained) layers for a particular task. Fine-tuning is performed on top of the pre-trained layers, which are preserved as the transformer's informational base. It is a procedure for customising the model to a particular domain and a set of applications.

Transformers can be efficiently trained by virtue of the fact that blocks of attention heads can be trained independently of each other and in parallel. Moreover, due to their normalisation layers and the fact that they retain information for all elements of the input throughout the encoding and decoding phases of processing, their architecture avoids both the vanishing and exploding gradient problems.

In addition, transformers can be trained on multi-modal data without revising their architecture. Their attention heads can recognise connections among text, visual images, and sound in the same way as they do among the terms of purely linguistic input.[9] This gives them considerably greater flexibility and power than earlier generations of DNNs.

Transformers constitute a significant breakthrough in deep learning. They are driving the large data models that have yielded the impressive results currently on display in many areas of AI. These include, *inter alia*, improved machine translation, strikingly natural text generation, improved speech recognition, effective image recognition, real-time video captioning, domain general question-answering, accurate medical diagnostics, pharmaceutical development, and code generation.

2.6 SOME WEAK ARGUMENTS AGAINST LARGE LANGUAGE MODELS

The large language models (LLMs) that transformers support are currently the focus of intense debate, both in the scientific disciplines where they have been developed and applied, and in the popular media. A variety of arguments have been brought against LLMs. Several of these lack substantial force, while others are compelling. In this section, I will briefly consider instances of the former. In Section 2.6, I will look at examples of the latter.[10]

Some critics assert that LLMs are "stochastic parrots" that do little more than return their training data. On this view, the fact that LLMs generate sentences, images, and sounds on the basis of the most probable continuations of data points to which they have already been exposed entails that they cannot go significantly beyond their training data in inferring structural regularities. Bender et al. (2021) and Chomsky et al. (2023) make versions of this claim. In fact, it is incorrect.

Transformers make surprising generalisations, and they recognise subtle patterns in new data, where these frequently elude humans. As we will see in Chapter 3, they identify abnormalities in X-rays, and they predict new molecular structures for proteins within the medical domain. They also learn complex new verbal commands in virtual environments, although these commands depart significantly from the linguistic data on which they have been trained. They identify scenes in graphic images, and they produce accurate descriptions for these scenes. They generate new computer code to solve difficult programming problems. The inferences that sustain these achievements cannot be reduced to simple variations of previously encountered regularities in data.

Bender and Koller (2020) argue that LLMs are incapable of capturing linguistic meaning, because they are trained entirely on text. Therefore, the semantic relations that they identify are corpus internal. They cannot recognise the connections between language and the world, and so they cannot properly interpret the expressions that they process or generate.[11] The argument is very limited in scope. It applies only to LLMs pre-trained on text alone. Transformers trained on both linguistic and non-linguistic data, like ViLBERT (Lu et al., 2019) and GPT-4 (OpenAI, 2023), have multi-modal embeddings that correlate linguistic and visual data (as well as sound, in the case of more recent LLMs). These embeddings ground text by specifying distributional patterns for words and phrases in non-linguistic environments.

OpenAI (2023) reports that ChatGPT-4 correctly describes a photo-graphic image of a cable connected to a contemporary smart phone with an old-fashioned VGA connector, commonly used for computer monitors. It replies to a question prompt asking about the humour of the photo by commenting on the absurdity of plugging an obsolete cable connector into the port for a small lightning connector in a modern phone. To the extent that this dialogue accurately represents the capacity of ChatGPT-4 to iden-tify elements and properties of previously unobserved images, it indicates considerable sophistication in its ability to interpret queries about visual scenes, and to infer conclusions about the objects in these scenes. It dem-onstrates complex semantic knowledge concerning language-world rela-tions of the kind that grounds linguistic meaning.

Marcus (2022) and Chomsky et al. (2023) criticise LLMs on the grounds that they fail to acquire grammars that encode linguistic knowledge as a set of rules and constraints. They argue that the absence of grammatical repre-sentations in a DNN prevents it from recognising the full range of accept-able linguistic structures, while ruling out ill-formed patterns. This criticism begs the scientific question under discussion. It assumes that linguistic knowledge must be expressed in symbolic form as a set of algebraic rules.

The fact that a DNN represents generalisations as configurations of weights assigned to elements of vectors, distributed through the units of a multi-layer processing system, does not entail that it is unable to achieve linguistic knowledge at a human level of accuracy. These configurations express the classification and prediction functions that the network learns from its training data. Some cognitive scientists, such as Smolensky (1987) and McClelland (2016), suggest that these distributed representations correspond to the way in which humans encode their knowledge of lan-guage and the world. Whether or not this is the case, the performance of recent LLMs on a variety of linguistic tasks indicates that they achieve implicit recognition of hierarchical syntactic structure, long-distance syn-tactic and semantic connections, and complex lexical semantic relations.[12]

Lappin (2021) and Baroni (2023) argue that DNNs should be considered as alternative models of linguistic knowledge.

I mentioned in Chapter 1 that Minsky (1991) suggests the need for hybrid systems that combine symbolic representations for rules (frames) with neural networks for learning. Marcus (2022) proposes a similar combination of DNNs with symbolic components. There have been a variety of attempts to integrate syntactic and semantic representations into deep learning. Most have not yielded significant improvements in performance in comparison with the corresponding DNN that is not enriched with these representations (Lappin, 2021, 2024), although at least one type of neuro-symbolic model does show considerable promise (Lappin, 2025). The efficacy of hybrid models remains an open question. Future research may discover effective methods for improving deep learning with the addition of rule-based components. But it may also be the case that the design of DNNs as distributed, vector encoding, parallel processing systems does not easily permit them to interpret and apply information when it is symbolically expressed in algebraic structures, like grammars and inference procedures.

It is important to see that the replies to the criticisms of LLMs considered in this section do not turn on the claim that transformers (or any other type of DNN) learn and represent knowledge in the same way that humans do. I am simply observing that they perform at or above human levels of accuracy on a wide range of cognitively interesting tasks, many of them within the area of NLP. The mechanisms that they use to do this may diverge from human learning and knowledge representation. We do not yet know enough about the neuroscience of human cognition to decide that question. Planes and helicopters fly through different engineering devices than the ones that birds apply (although all flight is governed by universal principles of aerodynamics). However, transformers do illuminate the nature of human learning, at least indirectly. They demonstrate what sorts of knowledge can, in principle, be effectively acquired from available data of a certain kind, with general learning systems that incorporate relatively weak, domain general, learning biases.

2.7 SOME STRONG ARGUMENTS ON THE LIMITATIONS OF LLMS

Piantadosi (2023) takes the ability of LLMs to learn intricate syntactic structure and semantic properties to overturn Chomsky's strong domain specific nativist view of language acquisition. He regards these systems as viable models of human learning. His claims go well beyond the available evidence. While the performance of LLMs indicates what types of knowledge can be acquired through domain general learning devices, their current achievements have not shown that transformers learn language in the way that humans do.

Warstadt and Bowman (2023) point out that LLMs are trained on considerably more data than human learners access during the acquisition process. Moreover, humans require social interaction and reinforcement for learning to occur, while LLMs do not. To test Piantadosi's assertions, it is necessary to restrict the data set and the training process for transformers to something resembling the environment in which children acquire language. This environment will contain far less data than transformers are currently exposed to. However, it will include reinforcement and language use in non-linguistic contexts, which may partially compensate for the reduction in linguistic data involved in replicating the human language acquisition environment.

A second limitation of LLMs concerns natural language inference (NLI), which involves inferring conclusions from premises on the basis of the lexical meanings of the expressions in the sentences. 2.2 is an example of such an inference. By contrast, 2.3 is not a case in which the conclusion follows from the premise.

2.2.   Premiss: Multiple males are playing soccer.
        Conclusion: Some men are playing a sport.
        Entailment

2.3.   Premiss: A smiling costumed woman is holding an umbrella.
        Conclusion: A happy woman in a fairy costume holds an umbrella.
        Non-entailment

When BERT is fine-tuned on existing NLI sets, such as the Stanford NLI corpus (Bowman et al., 2015), it does well on distinguishing entailments from non-inferences of various types in hold out test sets from these corpora. However, BERT is easily derailed by new test sets containing expressions that it has not encountered in its training data (Talman and Chatzikyriakidis, 2019). Moreover, BERT achieves unreasonably high test scores when fine-tuned and tested on nonsense sentences (Talman et al., 2021). Mahowald et al. (2024) present extensive evidence that LLMs do not do well on real-world reasoning tasks. Taken together, these results suggest that while transformers learn superficial patterns of inference and they are sensitive to some lexical semantic content in arguments, they do not acquire reliable deep reasoning abilities.

A third problem with LLMs is their tendency to generate fluent, plausible text which is entirely fictional. This is known as hallucination. As they produce expressions by successively selecting the next word with the highest probability value, given either the previous sequence of words, or the left and right contexts of the term in the input string, generation is not constrained by the factuality of the resulting sentence. This can create serious difficulties. In one instance, a lawyer who relied on ChatGPT-3 to find legal precedents unknowingly went to court with a set of fabricated cases to support his argument (Weiser, 2023).

LLM hallucination can undermine the reliability of question-answer systems and a variety of other applications. Devising effective procedures for verifying LLM output is a difficult and complex engineering challenge. Just checking this output against external sources does not ensure reliability. One problem is determining how closely the output needs to correspond to data in these sources. Exact match is far too restrictive a condition. But semantic similarity may be too permissive a requirement to filter out factually dubious LLM output. Establishing the factual grounding of the external sources is a second issue. Some of these sources may also contain fictional content in the form of text, images, or voice recording. Hallucination is related to the problem of deep fakes, which I take up in Chapter 5.

The opacity in the way that transformers (as well as earlier DNNs) achieve the generalisations that they learn poses a fourth significant problem. It is frequently the case that we are unable to identify the precise set of computations and procedures through which a transformer identifies a complex pattern in its training and input data. This is due to the fact the activation functions that it applies to its units, like ReLU, and the softmax function which returns a probability distribution over category judgements or predictions for its output, are non-linear. As a result, the relationship between its input and output vectors is, in general, not compositional. Consequently, it is not possible to predict a transformer's output vectors from the elements of its input vectors in a uniform and regular way. This follows from the absence of a homomorphic mapping between these vectors.[13] To the extent that transformers (and DNNs generally) are black boxes whose operations are not fully recognisable, we are not able to understand precisely how they learn and represent the knowledge that they acquire.

Indirect methods can illuminate the representations and internal information storage within a transformer. It is possible to train a probe to identify the abstract structures that transformers learn to identify. Hewitt and Manning (2019) develop a syntactic probe to discern the presence of dependency grammar trees in the processing that BERT and other transformers apply to several NLP tasks. We can also selectively turn off attention head blocks to observe the effect on a transformer's performance. Lasri (2023) uses this form of ablation to explore the types of syntactic knowledge that transformers acquire and to study how they are represented. While these procedures are useful, they remain indirect. They do not fully clarify the internal operations of deep learning in a transformer.[14]

Sections 2.6 and 2.7 are not intended to be an exhaustive presentation of the criticisms that have been raised against transformers. They provide a sense of the main problems that are being discussed with respect to this class of DNNs. As we saw in Section 2.6, some of the objections are not compelling. In the current section, we have taken up several of the more substantial difficulties that arise in connection with transformers and the LLMs that they support. In Chapter 3, we will look at a range of applications that these systems are being used for and some of the benefits that they are producing.

NOTES

1 The Google Cloud documentation *Introduction to Cloud TPU* (https://cloud.google.com/tpu/docs/intro-to-tpu) provides a brief explanation of CPUs, GPUs, and TPUs. It compares their designs, and their processing advantages, as well as their respective limitations. Kimm et al. (2021) present experimental comparisons of the three types of processors for a bidirectional LSTM on several deep learning tasks.

2 See Aaronson (2013) for an accessible and wide-ranging introduction to quantum computing.

3 See Pascanu et al. (2013) for a discussion of the vanishing and exploding gradient problems, and methods for avoiding them.

4 In Figure 2.2, σ is a sigmoid function, and tanh is a hyperbolic tangential function. See Lappin (2021) for brief explanations of these functions and discussions of different types of DNN in NLP.

5 On VSMs for lexical semantics, see Turney and Patel (2010), Lappin (2021), and Jurafsky and Martin (2023).

6 Jurafsky and Martin provide detailed explanations of skip gram and other embedding models.

7 See Jurafski and Martin for a clear introduction to self-attention and transformers.

8 For a sequence s consisting of tokens $w_1,...w_k$, this probability is computed according the formula $P(s) =$

$\prod^{|s|}_{i=0} P(w_i | w_{<i})$. Recent LLMs, like LLaMa (Touvron et al., 2023), developed by Meta, and the Mistral series (Jiang, 2023), are competitive in performance with ChatGPT models for several of the applications of the kind considered in Chapter 3. DeekSeek has released a series of models that achieve state of the art performance on many AI system metrics (DeepSeek-AI 2024a, 2024b, 2025), and they report substantial savings in training time and resources. It is important to note that the DeepSeek models are transformer driven LLMs, which employ the basic architecture of current systems. They make use of Reinforcement Learning to speed up training. However, they continue to use large numbers of parameters (236 billion parameters for DeepSeek V2, and 671 billion for V3), and substantial quantities of pre-training data (8.1 trillion tokens for V2 and 14.8 trillion for V3).

9 See Xu et al. (2023) for a survey of multi-modal transformers.

10 See Lappin (2024) for more detailed discussion of both types of argument.

11 This is an instance of Harnad's (1990) symbol grounding problem. It is also related to Searle's (1980) Chinese room argument.

12 See Lappin (2021), Goldberg (2019), Hewitt and Manning (2019), Wilcox et al. (2023), and Lasri (2023) for discussion of some of the experimental evidence for this claim.

13 A mapping $f: A \to B$ from group A to group B is a homomorphism iff for every $v_i, v_j \in A$, and the group operation $., f(A \cdot B) = f(A) \cdot f(B)$.

14 Bernardy and Lappin (2023) propose a fully transparent RNN, Unitary Recurrent Networks (URNs), as an alternative to current DNNs. URNs apply multiplication to orthogonal matrices of vectors to generate strictly compositional vectors as outputs. Therefore, an URN is fully transparent at each point in its computation. Inputs are recoverable from outputs at every phase of processing. While they are formally elegant, URNs are still limited in their accuracy. They achieve good results for deeply nested paranthesis matching tasks in artificial context-free languages. They do not perform well on cross-serial dependencies in mildly context-sensitive languages, or on number agreement for natural languages. One of their main limitations is their reliance on truncated matrices. Truncation involves removing matrix columns to reduce the size of the matrix rows. This technique is needed to maintain efficient processing, but it degrades the performance of the URN as the size and complexity of the input increase. Further research is necessary to deal with this issue.

CHAPTER 3

What Can Deep Neural Networks Do for Us?

To understand how recent advances in deep learning are having a substantial impact on the world that we live in, we need to look at some of the more prominent ways that it is driving the technology that we use. In this chapter, I will consider seven major domains in which the deep learning revolution has transformed our living and working environments. This is not intended to be an exhaustive list. I am offering a representative sample of applications in which transformers have radically changed the ways in which AI systems perform important real-world tasks. The purpose of these summary studies is to convey the range and diversity of technologies that now rely on deep neural networks (DNNs) as their main engines.

3.1 INFORMATION RETRIEVAL FOR Q&A

Information retrieval has traditionally involved identifying the documents that contain the answers to questions, and extracting the information that includes the answers, from these texts. Work in this area predates electronic computers, when it used a variety of mechanical techniques for coding and searching documents. With the advent of computers, it became a major area of scientific research and commercial development.[1]

The emergence of the internet in the 1990s provided instant access to large amounts of digital data, which required efficient online devices to navigate this rapidly expanding trove of content. Google, and other companies, emerged to provide search engines that indexed documents,

DOI: 10.1201/9781003624790-3

images, and videos, and ranked them in order of their relevance to users' queries. These initial devices were large-scale online information retrieval systems. They were specially keyed to the task of sorting digital content to match user queries. They relied largely on the statistical methods and the vector space models applied by the state-of-the-art information retrieval systems of the time for open domain queries on large text and image data bases.

Large language models (LLMs) are changing the design of information retrieval systems. As we saw in Chapter 2, they are pre-trained on very large multi-modal data bases, from which they extract their word embeddings. They can serve as question-answer chatbots without altering their architecture. They are able to generate fluent replies to questions, and they can produce content that does not correspond directly to the sentences or phrases in the documents from which they are deriving these answers. They do this by virtue of their capacity to recognise semantic similarity and paraphrase relations among distinct expressions. In some cases, they reach state of the art in the accuracy and quality of their replies to open domain questions. Kamalloo et al. (2023) show that when LLMs are assessed by human evaluation, rather than by automatic exact word/phrase matching metrics, their level of performance improves substantially. This is due to the fact that they frequently generate sentences containing words and phrases that do not occur in the gold standard replies extracted from the documents on which they are pre-trained.

In addition to relying on text to answer queries, multi-modal transformers are also able to access visual and voice data. They can describe graphic scenes and identify entities within them. They can read charts and graphs that represent quantitative information on a variety of topics. The multi-modal nature of current transformers significantly extends their power as information retrieval devices.

One of the problems that limits LLMs as Q&A systems is the fact that they can only access the information contained in the data on which they are pre-trained. Due to a time lag, this will invariably not be entirely up to date. Lewis et al. (2020) propose retrieval-augmented generation (RAG) to solve this (and other) difficulties. RAG is a procedure for fine-tuning transformers through accessing current online data to supplement their pre-trained embeddings. It permits them to generate answers that incorporate this information. RAG improves transformer accuracy in information retrieval tasks.

However, it does not entirely solve the problem of reliability. As we observed in Section 2.7, external online sources of data are not necessarily factual. Some of the text, images, and other data that RAG fine-tuning may rely on could be fictional, or otherwise unreliable. The issue of verification remains a significant challenge, which I will return to in Chapter 5.

3.2 MACHINE TRANSLATION

As we saw in Chapter 1, machine translation (MT) was one of the earliest applications of computers. The fact that initial MT systems were disappointingly limited in scope and accuracy was an important factor in producing the first AI winter.

The emergence of statistical MT (SMT; Brown et al., 1990; Jelinek, 1998) in the 1990s gave rise to wide coverage models that achieved significantly improved translation quality. These models were trained on large bilingual (or, in some cases, multilingual) corpora of aligned text. The first versions of SMT focused on word alignment in the source and target languages. A significant problem for MT is accommodating the lack of word-to-word correspondences between the sentence pairs that provide good translations. The Hebrew-English pairs in 3.1–3.2 illustrate this issue. 3.1(a)–3.2(a) give the Hebrew sentences with their literal word-by-word translation. 3.1(b)–3.2(b) are the corresponding correct English translations.

3.1 (a) Cham li.
hot to (clitic) me
(b) I am hot.

3.2 (a) Nichnas le-cheder, ve-hekir ota mi yad.
entered (3rd per sg m) to (clitic) room and recognised definite marker +clitic her from hand
(b) He entered the room, and he recognised her at once.

Moving from word-based to phrased-based SMT helped to alleviate this difficulty to some extent, by specifying probabilistic connections among larger syntactic units from each language. However, a component of the system devoted to handling sequence distortion and word order transformations was still required.[2]

SMT models were trained on large amounts of aligned parallel text in the languages between which translation was performed. The quality of the model and the translations that it produced depended on the availability of such data. Creating these data bases is an expensive, time-consuming enterprise.

With the move to deep learning-driven neural MT (NMT), the architecture shifted to an encoder-decoder framework. The encoder contains word embeddings for the source language, and the decoder for the target language. The entire model is pre-trained on large numbers of sentence pairs from each language. When attention is added to the context vector at the interface of the encoder and decoder, as in Bahdanau et al. (2015), the accuracy of translation is significantly improved. Transformers further enhance the precision of translation and the quality of generation, by permitting different sets of attention heads to learn distinct properties of sentence pairs relevant to translational correspondence.[3] These are seq2seq systems that do not require distortion or adjustment operations, or models, to generate appropriate target language sentences.

Han et al. (2021) propose an NMT architecture consisting only of a decoder generative model pre-trained on both source and target languages separately, rather than on parallel sentence pairs. When it is provided with a few high-quality examples of translation pairs from the two languages, the model quickly achieves state-of-the-art accuracy in translation. This system relies largely on unsupervised learning, and so it avoids the cost of an extensive training corpus of aligned text. It depends on LLMs from each of the two languages between which it translates. It learns the connections between the embeddings of these two models through a few well-constructed sentence pairs.

A decoder-only transformer which requires two LLMs cannot cover low-resource languages for which substantial training data is unavailable. Garcia et al. (2023) develop a decoder-only generative transformer, pre-trained on data from one language only, that can learn translation through a limited number of paired sentences that are used for fine-tuning. This approach shows promise of good performance through fine-tuning with sentences from a low-resource language. To the extent that it is successful, it will extend NMT to a much larger range of language pairs than are currently handled.

The rapid development of NMT over the past five years has resulted in the creation of high-performance translation systems that cover a greatly expanded set of languages. They are no longer limited to specialised areas, like technical manuals or news reports, as previous systems were. Instead, they yield increasingly accurate and natural translations for texts across a large spectrum of domains and styles. These systems are now widely available, at comparatively low cost (or free of charge), through the internet. NMT is one application in which deep learning has made substantial progress towards fulfilling the original promise of AI for fully automatic systems that learn from data to solve cognitively challenging tasks.

3.3 AUTOMATIC SPEECH RECOGNITION AND TEXT-TO-SPEECH GENERATION

Automatic speech recognition (ASR) and text to speech generation (TTS) have been important areas of study in AI and computer science from the beginnings of the field. Each of these tasks is, in effect, a version of the MT problem. How can a system accurately map expressions in a source language into corresponding terms of a target language? For ASR, the source consists of strings of speech sounds, while the target contains sequences of written words. TTS goes in the opposite direction.[4]

There are a variety of major challenges that efficient, accurate ASR has to address. It needs to generalise over different speakers whose voices operate at distinct ranges of pitch, volume, and tempo. It must also be able to accommodate varying pronunciations of the same set of words. Some of these divergences are due to regional dialects. Processing speech that is slow and delivered in a quiet environment is much easier than interpreting fast speech in a noisy context. The spoken output of a single speaker can be handled more straightforwardly than dialogue, where two or more speakers interact.

Notice that while a robust ASR model should be able to transcribe the speech of a wide range of sources, a TTS device needs to produce consistent output, simulating a single speaker. Also, a good TTS system will capture the rhythm, intonation patterns, and accent of natural human speech in a particular language. While TTS involves a mapping relation that is the inverse of ASR, the problems of producing acceptable output for each type of system are not identical.

The classic architecture for ASR is an encoder-decoder model. The encoder extracts phonetic features from spectrogram patterns of speech, and it encodes them as vectors. The decoder uses strings of feature vectors to condition the prediction of letters that form words. As in the case of SMT, older statistical ASR relied on large corpora of speech-word pairs to train probabilistic models to predict word sequences from speech streams. An influential version of this approach (Jelinek et al., 1975; Jelinek, 1995) applied HMMs (hidden Markov models, see Section 1.5) to build networks of probabilistic state transitions from which the model computes the likelihood of a word, given the phonetic features that have been received as input from the encoder, and the likelihood of the occurrence of the word (phrase, sentence), as determined by a language model.

DNNs have displaced devices like HMMs (hidden Markov models) for ASR and TTS. Initially, LSTMs and CNNs provided the encoder and decoder components. These earlier DNN models have now been largely surpassed by transformer-driven systems, as has happened with NMT.[5]

In Section 3.2, I pointed out that Han et al. (2021) propose an MT system that uses an LLM pre-trained on two or more languages, with supervised learning of a few high-quality examples of sentence pairings from source and target languages. This allows the transformer to operate as an MT system consisting only of a decoder. Fathullah et al. (2024) adopt a similar approach to ASR. They prefix the speech embeddings that a small voice encoder produces, directly to an LLM. The model is trained to generate text from speech embedding vectors. It is effectively a multimodal speech-to-text language model, and so it is a decoder-only ASR system. As it includes several text language models, it can perform multilingual speech recognition. This system improves on the accuracy of several baseline ASR models that it is compared with. Le et al. (2023) describe a generative model of TTS that works across languages for rapid learning of speech production.

Current ASR and TTS systems support a variety of important applications, which are now pervasive in our working and leisure environments. Dictation programs that transcribe spoken input to text on mobile phones and other devices are a prominent instance of a widely used ASR application. Spoken dialogue management is common in businesses and government offices, handling at least the initial phases of customer telephone calls. ASR is also applied by airlines, and other types of company, for telephone bookings. Automatic captioning of videos and television broadcasts rely on ASR. Speech-to-speech MT uses both ASR and TTS. Verbal satnav systems apply TTS, as do automatic text readers for people with limited or no vision.

Many of these applications were developed decades ago with statistical language and processing models. As transformers and powerful new hardware have become available, these applications have greatly improved in accuracy and computational efficiency. They have also started to converge on human performance and, in some cases, to surpass it.

3.4 CODE GENERATION

Software engineering has traditionally involved programmers writing programs with many lines of code in one or more computer languages. This code has to be carefully debugged to remove errors, and it has to be optimised to run efficiently. This is a labour-intensive process, which involves a fair amount of repetitive work. Deep learning has been gradually eliminating the lower-level tasks of coding by allowing for increasingly accurate, wide coverage automatic code assessment, correction, and generation.

Code generation can be formulated as an instance of the MT task. Natural language text is mapped into expressions in a computer language. Recent work has used transformers to implement this mapping in the same way that they are applied to translation between source and target natural languages.[6] As in the case of MT systems, encoder-decoder and decoder-only architectures are used. In the former, the transformer is pre-trained on large amounts of paired natural language and code data, where much of the natural language text consists of comments on the code. In the generation only framework language models are constructed for both text and code. A few supervised examples of pairings between expressions from each model are used to fine-tune the system to generate code and to correct it. If the transformer includes several coding language models, then it can generate code across these languages.

To the extent that it is possible to automate the generation, correction, and optimisation of code, software engineers can use LLMs as coding assistants that free them from much of the labour of writing and testing programs. They can devote their time and creativity to higher-level architectural questions of system design and development. This is a case in which deep learning AI can seriously contribute to the enhancement of productivity and efficiency in a core engineering discipline.

3.5 AUTOMATIC THEOREM PROVING

Theorem proving has been an important area of research in AI since the 1950s. As mathematical results have become increasingly complex and difficult to assess manually, these systems have attracted growing interest among mathematicians. Early work used rule-based procedures to generate and test proofs of statements in logic and mathematics. Each procedure was constructed for a specific formal system. They were often computationally expensive and inefficient. They did not learn from data, but they applied proof algorithms to statements in a mathematical or logical language.[7]

Current neural theorem provers consist of LLMs pre-trained on large data sets of proofs, some of them annotated for correctness. They are designed to generate probability distributions for a range of possible continuations (subgoals) of a proof, and they select the most highly valued one. Training involves the same sorts of backpropagation and loss functions that are applied to learning for other tasks. The state-of-the-art performance of some of these models is encouraging, and they are able to handle proofs in a variety of mathematical and logical systems.[8]

Neural theorem provers contribute to mathematical work in at least three ways. First, they can, in general, prove theorems more efficiently, quickly, and reliably than humans. Second, they may discover shorter, more efficient proofs of statements than those that human mathematicians have managed to construct. Finally, they can be used as proof assistants to check the correctness of human proofs and to correct mistakes in existing proof claims.

It is important to recognise that these applications are useful not only for theoretical research in logic and mathematics. Scientific theories and engineering work frequently depend on the correctness of certain formal results for their viability. Efficient wide coverage automatic theorem provers and proof assistants facilitate the process of producing and checking these results. Recent advances in deep learning have greatly enhanced the coverage and the efficiency of automatic theorem proving and assessment.

3.6 MEDICAL AND BIOINFORMATIC APPLICATIONS

DNNs have become an important tool in the diagnosis and treatment of a wide variety of medical conditions. They are applied to problems of image classification to identify abnormalities and pathologies in single organs and for sets of organs.[9] In previous phases of this work, Convolutional Neural Networks (CNNs) were the primary devices applied to image recognition tasks. While these are effective in fine-grained pattern identification within small areas, they are limited in their capacity to recognise connections among disparate parts of images separated by large distances.

Visual transformers support classification in these larger image contexts more successfully, and they tend to outperform CNNs in many diagnostic tasks. However, they require large training data sets, as well as fine-tuning, and they are computationally more expensive than CNNs. As a result, hybrid systems that interpolate CNN and transformer layers are often used to optimise performance and resource requirements. DNNs now outperform human diagnosticians in accuracy on a number of recognition tasks. They also achieve results more quickly. Visual transformers are used to enhance low-resolution visual images obtained from fMRI (functional magnetic resonance imaging) and ultrasound scans. This improves the interpretability of the images and facilitates more accurate assessment of a patient's condition.

Multi-modal transformers are employed to generate written medical reports from images. This is a version of the MT task where the source language consists of visual representations, and the target comprises sentences and phrases in natural language. Related to this task is the production of instructions for surgical and other sorts of treatment from a categorised set of images. Training a transformer on a multi-modal data set containing text (or speech) and images permits a higher level of performance in both diagnosis and treatment recommendations.

Transformers have also revolutionised the prediction of protein properties in bioinformatics and computational biology. Using individual amino acids as word-type units, and amino acid sequences as the counterparts of sentences (or phrases), they extract embeddings from large protein databases. These encode the distributional features of acids within proteins. Transformers are pre-trained to create protein "language" models. They can be fine-tuned on annotated data sets for specific tasks. Both autoregressive and masked token BERT-type models are employed for many bioinformatic applications. They handle some of these tasks as variants of MT, where an encoded input protein sequence is mapped to a decoded output sequence. For others, they classify proteins as of a particular type. Transformers also identify correlations between protein types and elements of proteins through regression analysis. They yield state-of-the-art results, and they significantly improve performance over Recurrent Neural Networks (RNNs) and Convolutional Neural Networks (CNNs) in most instances. However, hybrid systems achieve optimal effects for some cases.[10]

Transformers predict structural properties of proteins, and they identify long-distance relations between widely separated elements of protein sequences in large molecular contexts. This permits the recognition of abnormalities in cells. It also allows them to anticipate the effects of viruses and bacteria on proteins in cells and to assign probability distributions to the effects of different sorts of medication. They can project the patterns of protein evolution due to genetic changes. Transformers predict the properties of novel protein sequences. This has made them a powerful assistant in the development of innovative pharmacological treatments. They are also becoming increasingly significant in applications within computational biology, where they are useful for modelling patterns of cell development and genetic change.

3.7 MUSIC AND FINE ARTS

Deep learning systems are employed to generate musical compositions in a variety of genres. As with the other applications that we have considered here, RNNs and CNNs have given way to LLMs supported by transformers. These are able to track dependencies over longer distances across a piece, where musical coherence requires that these connections be maintained throughout extended sequences of notes and bars.

Transformers are trained on large numbers of compositions from which they extract embeddings of notes and other musical units. These compositions are represented in symbolic formats like Musical Instrument Digital Interface (MIDI), which specify the sound features of notes.[11] These representations are mapped back into sounds. The embeddings are encoded as vectors. A musical transformer will, in most cases, generate a symbolic representation of a new composition from its input. It can do this through an encoder-decoder architecture, where it receives an initial prompt or musical theme as encoded input, and it produces a piece as the predicted continuation of this prefix as its decoded output. Alternatively, it can generate its composition directly through a decoder-only architecture, as in the case of some of the MT systems that we looked at.

Achieving structural coherence, melodic richness, and rhythmic consistency is a significant challenge in musical generation. The initial theme of a piece can get lost as the length of the composition increases. Shih et al. (2022) propose a transformer that tracks musical themes throughout compositions to deal with this problem. Their model is designed for single instrument pieces, particularly those played on a piano. Dong et al. (2023) present a multitrack transformer that generates compositions for orchestral ensembles involving a variety of instrument and vocal combinations.

Most musical transformers are autoregressive. They predict the next note on the basis of the sequence that precedes it. They may require a non-empty musical prefix as a prompt to initiate the generation process. Alternatively, some systems can produce a composition from an empty start note symbol. Sarmento (2024) describes both unconditioned and conditional models that generate guitar pieces in tablature representation.

He also reports several experiments in interactive composition in which human musicians modify a model-generated theme to produce a final song.

Current state-of-the-art musical transformers score well on both objective performance metrics and human evaluation. In many cases, they approach the assessments that people assign to original human compositions of the same type. It is important to recognise that these systems are not reproducing compositions that they are trained on, and so they are not simply imitating this data. They are generating original pieces of music, some of which exhibit innovative features, across a cluster of genres.

DNNs also generate images for films and other artistic productions. However, one of the important emerging applications of deep learning in the fine arts involves classification and discrimination, rather than generation. DNNs are becoming increasingly influential as devices for determining artist attribution and authentication of paintings. The former task involves determining which artist, among a set of candidates, is responsible for a specific work. The latter requires a binary decision between the authenticity of a painting for a particular artist and its production by another painter. This distinction is difficult to make for high-quality forgeries and for works painted in a similar style to that of the original artist.

In the case of attribution, a DNN is trained on a labelled data set of originals by different artists. The model assigns a probability distribution, conditioned by the pixel patches of the painting that it receives as input, over the candidate artists for which it has been trained. For authentication, the model is trained on a set of images that is partitioned into two labelled sets of images: one containing work by the original artist and the second with paintings by others, which resemble the originals in style and genre. For visual transformers, which are pre-trained on a large corpus of images, the partitioned data set is used for fine-tuning.

Schaerf et al. (2023) compare two CNNs with two variants of a visual transformer for accuracy in distinguishing between original works by van Gough and similar paintings by different artists. They train all four models on a large data base of images, which are segmented into patches of pixels. Both the CNNs and the transformers achieve reasonably high accuracy on several discrimination tasks, with the transformer outperforming the CNNs in identifying similar non-van Gough paintings.

Chen et al. (2023) test a hybrid CNN + visual transformer model on classification of Chinese paintings by a particular artist and a set of similar non-authentic images. This task poses problems not encountered with most traditional Western painting due to the presence of large quantities of empty, or sparsely filled, space in the Chinese work. Their model incorporates a procedure for identifying those patches of pixels that are more central to classification of the painting and increasing their weights. The experiments that they report indicate that the model does well in recognising similar non-original images.

Prior to deep learning, most AI systems were task-specific. They were designed for a particular set of applications in a given domain. In order to apply them to different objectives, it was necessary to completely reconfigure them, often with new handcrafted rules or features. As we have seen with the applications considered in this chapter, it is possible to apply DNNs, particularly transformers, to many different kinds of tasks, while retaining the same basic architecture. The transformers that support LLMs are the current state of the art for DNNs. Although they were initially developed for applications in NLP, they are now being employed for non-linguistic and multi-modal tasks and domains of the kind sampled in this chapter. The fact that a general architecture is able to sustain learning and yield high-performance across such a wide range of objectives is the key to the power and flexibility of deep learning models. It is one of the major factors that has produced the current revolution in AI.

NOTES

1 See Sanderson and Croft (2012) for a brief history of information retrieval, and Grishman (2010) for a discussion of pre-DNN computational methods of information extraction.

2 See Way (2010) for a discussion of phrase-based SMT.

3 Stahlberg (2020) provides a history of NMT from RNNs and CNNs to transformers.

4 See Jurafsky and Martin (2023) for an overview of ASR and TTS systems.

5 See Wang et al. (2021) and Kim et al. (2022) for transformer-based ASR, and Zhang et al. (2023) for transformers in TTS.

6 Atkinson (2023) discusses code generation and correction for Python with application to a particular software problem. He focusses on using prompts for ChatGPT-3.5 to produce and check the relevant code. Espejel et al. (2023) review the application of LLMs to generating Java code. Soliman et al. (2024) propose a hybrid transformer model for code generation.

7 See, for example, Fitting (1996) on the implementation of resolution and tableaux theorem provers for first-order logic.

8 See Plou and Sutskever (2020), Lample et al. (2022), and Yang et al. (2023) for examples of transformer-based theorem provers and proof assistants.

9 Shamshad et al. (2023) provide a wide-ranging survey of recent and contemporary work on the use of CNNs and transformers for visual image classification and interpretation in medical domains.

10 Chandra et al. (2023) give a useful review of recent work on deep learning and the role of transformers in protein prediction for applications in bioinformatics and computational biology.

11 Sarmento (2024) describes several models for generating tablature representations for guitar compositions.

CHAPTER 4

Risks Imagined

4.1 VISIONS OF THE SINGULARITY

I noted in Chapter 1 that Turing (1950) wisely avoided suggesting a precise definition of general intelligence. We do not have a clear scientific understanding of this property, and it is not obvious that we will ever be able to achieve it. Instead, he proposed the Turing test as an operational criterion for identifying intelligent behaviour in a machine. In the same paper, he anticipates that we would construct machines that are reasonable candidates for passing the test by the end of the twentieth century. It is important to recognise that Turing does not predict the creation of general machine intelligence by this or any other date. He foresees the advent of computational systems that we would be prepared to describe as "thinking". He expresses this view as a careful and qualified observation on the accepted use of language.

> I believe that in about 50 years' time it will be possible to programme computers, with a storage capacity of about 10^9 to make them play the imitation game so well that an average interrogator will not have more than 70%, chance of making the right identification after five minutes of questioning. The original question, "Can machines think!" I believe to be too meaningless to deserve discussion. Nevertheless, I believe that at the end of the century the use of words and general educated opinion will have altered so much that one will be able to speak of machines thinking without expecting to be contradicted (p. 442).

DOI: 10.1201/9781003624790-4

Other thinkers have been considerably less restrained. They have predicted a *singularity*, a point in history in which machine intelligence surpasses human cognitive abilities, and the world is transformed as a result. The term seems to have originated with von Neumann. In a memorial article, Ulam (1958) cites him as regarding the trajectory of rapid technological change as leading to a juncture at which the conditions of human life are radically altered.

> One conversation centered on the ever accelerating progress of technology and changes in the mode of human life, which gives the appearance of approaching some essential singularity in the history of the race beyond which human affairs, as we know them, could not continue.

Interestingly, the quote does not specifically identify the singularity with the growth of computational intelligence.

The mathematician and computer scientist I.J. Good (1966) offers one of the first detailed speculative descriptions of the process through which a superintelligent computer would emerge. He takes the exponential increase in computing, storage, and memory capacity as allowing for the development of massively parallel neural networks connected to large data sets. These devices will integrate inference and reasoning in a way that achieves intelligent machines that can improve their own designs. This will initiate a process through which each generation of computers will create a more powerfully intelligent successor. He predicts the creation of the first ultra-intelligent device by the end of the twentieth century.

While Good acknowledges the acute risks that superintelligent machines could pose, he also regards them as essential to human survival and progress. He suggests that they could solve serious health and social problems, and they may provide a way of escaping the planet/galaxy, when it can no longer support life in the distant future.

Vinge (1993) also expects the singularity in the near future. In addition to the rapid rise of powerful hardware, he takes computer networks, like the internet, and the combination of human brains with microchips, as other factors that may cause computational systems to "come alive" as intelligent agents. Vinge sees this process as inevitable, and not subject to prevention. He warns of the dangers that it poses, but also recognises its possible benefits. He reflects on options for encoding safety constraints in intelligent computers.

The futurist Ray Kurzweil (1999, 2006) imagines an elaborate and far-reaching version of the singularity. He uses Moore's law on the exponential growth of microchip capacity to argue that the rise of computing power will continue until it far surpasses that of the human brain. Moore (1965), an electronic engineer and one of the co-founders of the microchip company Intel, initially asserted that the number of transistors etched on a microchip would double every year, and he subsequently revised this time frame to every 18 months to 2 years. The corrected prediction has been shown to be roughly accurate over a 60-year period. The result has been an exponential rise in the computing power of central processing unit (CPU) chips.

The graph that represents the exponential increase in Intel CPU processing capacity is generated by the exponential function $ML(t_k)$, defined by the formula $ML(t_k) = t_i * 2^y$, where t_k = the number of transistors at time k, t_i = the number of transistors at time i ($i < k$), and y = the number of 2-year (or 18 month) periods between i and k.[1]

Kurzweil claims that exponential patterns of this kind are pervasive in the natural order, particularly in biological evolution, as well as in social domains. Human evolution occurred quickly, and then effectively moved to technological change. He acknowledges that CPU expansion cannot maintain exponential growth indefinitely due to physical constraints. But he anticipates that alternative hardware designs, like graphics processing units (GPUs), tensor processing units (TPUs), and qubits, will sustain the momentum of development.

As part of the singularity, Kurzweil envisages the increasing interaction of electronic chips and human brains through insertion of the former in the latter. He also speculates on the rise of a nanotechnology in which intelligent micro-robots are introduced into the human body for medical purposes, and to enhance perceptual and cognitive functions. He postulates that it will be possible, in the foreseeable future, to upload one's entire mental identity, as encoded in one's brain, into an electronic system. He shares the concerns of other singularity theorists over the dangers posed by the sort of technology that he describes. However, he holds what seems to be a basically optimistic view of its potential benefits in eradicating food shortages and poverty, freeing people from repetitive labour, resolving conflict, and improving human health. Ultimately, he regards it as a route to mental immortality through emancipation from biological embodiment.

Interesting as these speculations on the singularity may be, they appear to rest on at least two highly questionable assumptions. The first is the claim that computing power will continue to grow at an exponential rate. In fact, contrary to Kurzweil's claim, most patterns in both the natural and the social world tend not to be permanently exponential, even when

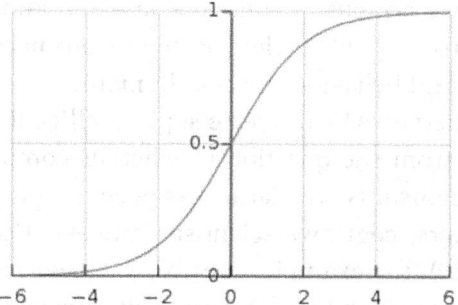

FIGURE 4.1   Sigmoid function (= Figure 1.2).

exhibiting phases of sharp expansion. In biological evolution, for example, most species, after reaching a certain level of adaptation and viability, tend to become stable over a long period of time. Even many species of higher primates have survived in their contemporary form over several million years. Similarly, populations of a species often grow very quickly, and then level off. This plateauing effect appears to be happening with human population expansion now.

New technologies frequently develop very quickly, and then stabilise at a steady state, once they mature. Most new aircraft currently in use exhibit only minor modifications of designs and technologies that have existed for well over half a century. This pattern of development seems closer to the function whose S-shaped graph we see in Figure 4.1. The sigmoid function that generates the graph in Figure 4.1 is a logistic function, defined by the formula $S(x) = e^x/e^x + 1$.

But even if we accept the view that computing hardware will continue to enjoy an exponential increase in power over the long-term future, this does not entail the emergence of superintelligence. The relevant sort of intelligence cannot be simply reduced to vast computing resources.

While continuing to remain within Turing's operational approach, we can identify at least three features of behaviour that are indicative of general intelligence. These need not be taken as necessary or sufficient conditions. They are best thought of as marks or symptoms of intelligent ways of functioning. First, an intelligent agent is goal directed. He/she/it pursues an objective in a purposeful way. Second, the agent is volitional. It chooses its goals and the ways that it achieves them. Finally, it employs rational methods of planning and implementation to realise these objectives over a wide range of domains. It is not restricted to a limited set of tasks or applications in its reasoning power. Rationality includes efficient use of resources and systematic, consistent planning strategies. I am specifically excluding subjective notions of consciousness, self-awareness, sentience, and emotion in this account, as there is no obvious need to treat them as elements of intelligent behaviour for non-humans.

The issue of whether AI can create superintelligent machines should be distinguished from the question of whether computational devices can achieve consciousness. The latter has been a topic of intense debate among philosophers, cognitive scientists, and AI theorists over many years. Searle (1980), for example, uses his Chinese room argument to claim that this is, in principle, not possible. By contrast, Chalmers (1996) identifies minds and consciousness with invariant organisational structure and causal patterns in computation. He maintains that artificial devices can acquire conscious mental states if they achieve a certain level of computational functionality. He identifies this notion of mental activity with the strong AI thesis, which he defends. Unlike Chalmers, I have construed this thesis to assert not the possibility of conscious mental states in computational systems but the prospect of arriving at general rationality in the sense that I have sketched here. I am suggesting that whether or not computational devices are conscious or self-aware is entirely orthogonal (and ultimately irrelevant) to the problem of superintelligence.

Notice that the three marks of intelligence that I have enumerated are all emergent properties of physical systems, particularly of the human brain. We can, at most, discern correlations between specific patterns of neural activity and intelligent behaviour that displays these features in particular environments.[2]

Now consider Kurzweil's second assumption. He is persuaded that we will be able to reproduce the structure and computational activity of a human brain in the circuitry of an advanced computational system. He seems to suggest that this will produce intelligence in the system. If this is, in fact, his view, it is unsound. As we have just observed, the features of human intelligence that I have proposed as marks of general intelligent behaviour are emergent. They cannot be directly reduced to the circuitry of the brain or of an electronic device. There is no reason to expect the properties to emerge from any computer that we construct, no matter how vast its computational power may be, or how closely it resembles the design of the brain.

Computers are already far more powerful than brains in their storage capacity and their computing speed, as well as in their accuracy of computation. They are designed for engineering performance, not for analogy to human neural systems. In this respect, they resemble aircraft, which are optimised for aerodynamic efficiency, rather than to resemble birds or other flying creatures. It simply does not follow that by adding computational power and closer approximation to human neural activity, the emergent properties of intelligent behaviour will suddenly appear.

The notion of the singularity remains a logical possibility. We may, at some point in the future, create computational agents that exhibit intelligence in the sense indicated here. However, no current AI system comes close to achieving these properties, however impressive its performance may be on the tasks for which it is effective. These systems are not in any way either volitional or rational in a domain general way. In Section 2.7, we noted that while current LLMs do very well on a wide range of NLP applications, their performance on natural language inference is weak. Mahowald et al. (2023) present extensive evidence that they have significant difficulties in handling real-world reasoning.[3] Moreover, it is not clear how foreseeable developments of current systems could achieve the properties that we identify with intelligent agency. The singularity is, then, an interesting thought experiment of imaginative futurists, rather than an imminent prospect.[4]

4.2 SUPERINTELLIGENT AGENTS AS AN EXISTENTIAL THREAT

An increasingly prominent theme in recent popular discussion of AI portrays superintelligence as a long-term existential threat to human survival. Yudkowsky (2008) sketches a variety of scenarios in which a destructive set of AI agents emerge in an "explosion of intelligence" that threatens human survival. He suggests that the only effective way to avoid such a situation is to ensure that AI agents are designed as intrinsically benevolent to respect and promote human well-being. He refers to this type of superintelligence as *friendly AI*.

Bostrom (2014) presents a detailed case for the view that superintelligent artificial agents are likely at some point in the future. He argues that, unless they are properly constrained, they will constitute an acute risk to human survival. Like Vinge and Kurzweil, he cites the rapid expansion of computational power, the exponential increase in biological evolution leading to the emergence of human intelligence, combined with technological augmentation, brain emulation, and the rise of integrated computer networks, as alternative possible lines through which superintelligence could appear. He concludes that the existence of these alternative routes to superintelligence renders its emergence highly likely.

Bostrom amplifies some of the ideas of the earlier singularity theorists considered in Section 4.1 to offer scenarios for the way in which superintelligent agents will behave. Specifically, he sees them as pursuing objectives with an efficiency of planning and of methods that far surpass human capacities. These may well be entirely incompatible with human concerns and well-being. He also suggests that it is highly likely that superintelligence will be concentrated in a single unified agent that relentlessly increases its own computational capacity and intelligence through successive cycles of self-improvement (although he does allow for a multiplicity of such agents). Unless current work on AI is properly planned to take account of the likelihood of superintelligence, this agent will not be amenable to human control, and it will elude attempts to constrain it.

Bostrom illustrates the threat that superintelligence poses to human survival with several examples. In one case, an AI system that has as its objective the testing of the Riemann hypothesis (a mathematical conjecture concerning a class of functions) turns the entire solar system into a computing device to facilitate its research, destroying the planet in the process. In a second case, an AI agent that seeks to produce a maximal number of paperclips uses large parts of the solar system (and beyond) as resources in its production process, again ruining life on Earth. He reflects at length on ways of avoiding these kinds of eventualities by programming AI technology with appropriate objectives that exclude destructive robotic behaviour.

Bostrom's speculations do not assume that the singularity is imminent, or that it will develop directly out of current AI models. He acknowledges that superintelligence could be at a considerable distance in the future. He recognises that it may require major changes in AI systems that are some way off. Bostrom also grants that superintelligence could provide a variety of beneficial improvements to human life. His focus, however, is to warn of the dire threats that it poses, and to urge that proper planning to deal with these dangers be incorporated into AI research now.

To what extent do we need to regard these warnings on the dangers of AI superintelligence as well motivated and pressing? As I noted in Section 4.1, the main markers of general intelligence are emergent properties of physical systems, like the brain. They cannot be reduced to mechanisms and patterns in these systems. Nor are they simply collective features of these physical systems, achieved through their constituents, in the way that computational actions are performed by the collections of electronic circuits which make up microprocessors. Volition, planning, and domain general reasoning are properties of humans (and other organisms) that go well beyond the biological hardware with which they are realised.

Bostrom, like the singularity theorists who preceded him, sees intelligence as emerging out of the increasing power and complexity of computational devices, some of which he anticipates as fully emulating human brain functions. At no point do these theorists explain how volition, planning, and purposeful behaviour will emerge from complex electronic circuitry on its own. The fact that we have evolved to exhibit intelligence and that we have achieved it through cortical activity in our brain does not entail that we can reproduce it by building powerful electronic computing systems, even if these resemble brains in important functional aspects. This crucial explanatory gap undermines every account of superintelligence that I have encountered to date.

In his review of Bostrom's book, Searle (2014) claims that artificial superintelligence is not possible, because machines are incapable of conscious states. This is, in effect, an application of his Chinese room argument to the question of general AI. Häggström (2016) dismisses Searle's criticism on the grounds that mental states of the sort that humans experience are not a necessary condition for intelligence. The internal computational states of an artificial agent may be sufficient to drive behaviour that we recognise as intelligent in the relevant sense. In proposing an operational approach to general intelligence which does not rely on attributing consciousness to an intelligent agent, we have adopted a similar approach to Häggström on this issue. His rejection of Searle's critique of Bostrom is well motivated.

However, while this may dispose of consciousness as a relevant consideration in the discussion, it does not solve the problem of explaining how the identifying emergent properties of general intelligence can suddenly appear in an artificial network of electronic circuits. Pointing to functional analogies with the human brain does not fill this lacuna. No such properties have emerged from powerful complex computational devices to date, and it is not obvious how they might do so in the future.

It is, of course, necessary to concede that such an emergence is, in principle, possible. But none of the advocates of superintelligence have given us any reason to believe that it is likely now or in the foreseeable future. Nor have they shown that it is reasonable to expect that current AI systems, or readily imaginable modifications of them, will yield the properties of general intelligence which we have described. Instead, they have pointed out that the power of computational technology and the simulation of biological systems, particularly of brains, are both developing rapidly. While these observations are correct, they do not support the claim that artificial general intelligence is on the horizon. Therefore, this seems to be a clear case of inferring the conclusion that an event is probable from the premiss that it is logically possible. This is not a persuasive argument, and we should resist it.

4.3 ASSESSING AND PRIORITISING RISK

In order to respond rationally to risks, it is necessary to assess both their likelihood and their gravity. Superintelligent agents would be a potentially serious threat if they appeared, given the damage that they could do to humanity. Bostrom, Häggström, and others have imagined the nature of this destruction in some detail. The main problem, then, is to evaluate the likelihood of the danger coming to pass within the foreseeable future. This task is complicated by the fact that superintelligence, or even general intelligence at a human level, in an artificial device, has never been observed. We are, then, required to assess the likelihood of a previously unseen event.

There are well-developed formal tools in probability theory for assigning values to unobserved classes and phenomena. I noted in Chapter 1 that Good (1953) published the Good-Turing smoothing procedure for giving non-nil probability to previously unobserved population classes. I also described how Bayesian HMMs (hidden Markov models) can be used to predict unseen word classes. Kneser-Ney smoothing (Kneser and Ney, 1995) is a backoff method used to predict the probability distribution of n-grams in a text. It will determine probabilities for n-grams not observed in that text. All of these methods (and others) rely on similarity relations between observed events, whose frequencies can be measured, and unobserved events, with no frequency of occurrence. These similarities support prediction by comparison with known classes of phenomena.

The emergence of superintelligence in artificial agents does not resemble any previously known event. Therefore, the techniques of probability theory for predicting the likelihood of previously unseen phenomena do not appear to be applicable to this case. We are not able to quantify its likelihood as a conditional probability, even very roughly, in any formally credible way. It stands in marked contrast to risks like atmospheric carbon-induced climate change, for which the likelihood of its occurrence within a specified time frame can be predicted with measurable accuracy. We can also evaluate the dangers associated with climate change, given the known causal connections between steadily increasing temperatures and a wide variety of environmental effects, such as rising sea levels due to melting glaciers, and increased rainfall or drought, in different geographical regions.

Häggström acknowledges that the probability of superintelligent agents cannot be quantified as a precise prediction. He does, however, insist that it is a very likely development. He suspects that it will occur by the end of the current century. His main reasons for this claim are versions of those already advanced by Bostrom and earlier singularity theorists. These include the following four developments, three of which I mentioned in previous subsections. First, the computing power of hardware has increased exponentially over the past 60 years, and it is continuing to follow this trajectory. Second, computational networks have expanded rapidly, and they have become highly integrated, with access to vast amounts of data and software. Third, software methods like genetic algorithms that project development over many generations of agents permit us to simulate the biological evolutionary processes that resulted in human cognition and intelligence. Finally, we are approaching the point where we will be able to accurately model high-order functions of the brain through computational systems.

Let us consider these in turn. Computing power does not, in itself, generate intelligent behaviour of the required variety, although it may be a necessary condition for it. We have already observed that current computers far surpass the computing and memory capacities of humans, but they remain free of general intelligence. Why will adding more power to these systems cause them to exhibit such intelligence? Networks like the internet are substantial tools for communication, computation, and accessing data. Once again, how do their power and complexity suddenly give rise to the properties of general intelligence? Genetic algorithms, and other simulation techniques, allow us to construct real-time models of biological development. They do not reproduce biological evolution, nor do they model the processes through which intelligence, rather than human brains, has emerged. Similarly, modelling brain functions in electronic circuits does not entail the emergence of intelligence or cognition.

In general, Bostrom, Häggström, and other singularity theorists cite the physical and structural factors enumerated above as drivers of general intelligence, without showing significant correlations between these factors and the emergent properties of intelligence. More significantly, they do not propose plausible mechanisms through which these properties would emerge from electronic circuits of the kind that currently sustain computation or that we can envisage in the near future.

Consider the deep neural networks (DNNs) that have mastered challenging games of strategy, like chess or Go, to the point that they can defeat any human opponent. They have been trained on human data to learn to compute sequences of moves that achieve a specified result. Their computational power and their memories permit them to test in parallel a far larger number of possible interactive move sequences, much more rapidly, than any human player can. They are able to select the most highly valued move from among the many sequences that they represent, and so they win against a human player. There is no volition in their actions. The DNN is generating a probability distribution over move sequences, and it selects the optimal one at each stage of the game. This is a domain specific skill. Even when it is transferred to other tasks (in zero or few shot learning), like computing the shortest path through a set of points in a graph, it does not generalise to innovative reasoning across domains. Therefore, it does not resemble the volitional, goal-directed, domain general behaviour that we identify with human intelligence.

Such intelligence may arise in computational devices in the future. However, singularity theorists have not given us any basis for understanding how this will happen. They have also not offered us a substantive reason to expect its occurrence in the near or intermediate future. In general, it is advisable to prioritise risks in terms of the likelihood and immediacy of the threats that they pose. Climate change, rising economic inequality, political extremism, pandemics, and geopolitical instability, among others, seem to be more pressing dangers than superintelligence. As such, they would appear to be more acute priorities for remedial action than the prospect of superintelligent artificial agents.

4.4 AUTONOMOUS CONTROL DEVICES VS INTELLIGENT ARTIFICIAL AGENTS

It is important to distinguish intelligent artificial agents from the general class of technology that controls a range of processes automatically through external feedback. Automatic control devices have existed since antiquity. A simple instance is a thermostat which activates a heater when its temperature gage drops below a certain point, and which turns on an air conditioner when it goes above another level. Its operation is fully autonomous in that it requires no human intervention. It is conditioned by the temperature of the room in which it is located.[5]

A more interesting example is the automatic pilot that operates a commercial aircraft for much of its flight. Engineers of the Sperry Corporation in the United States designed the first autopilot in 1912, and they demonstrated it in 1914. This device used a gyroscope to stabilise the plane's flight and trajectory. Later systems added additional instruments, like altimeters, to provide richer data input and additional aspects of flight control. Current systems rely on software to navigate the flight course and a range of instruments to measure the plane's position and movement. They are connected to the aircraft's hydraulic mechanism to regulate engine thrust, wing flaps, and the tail rudder in order to maintain the flight course and the right altitude. They also correct for a variety of forces, such as wind and pressure. While human pilots normally handle take-off and landing, automatic systems can also handle these parts of the journey.

While automatic control devices are fully autonomous, they clearly do not exhibit intelligence in the sense relevant to the issue of superintelligent artificial agents. They are in no sense volitional, and they do not learn. They perform a limited set of pre-programmed operations conditioned by external stimuli. They can also pose serious safety threats, if they are not well designed or properly used.

Autonomous weapons are a particular source of concern. They may fire indiscriminately at targets when activated by senor input or heat readings. They can do enormous damage to innocent people through faulty targeting or unconstrained design. Automatic systems that control dams over large rivers, traffic flow, food processing, pharmaceutical manufacturing, etc. all create complex safety issues. Like autopilots, these are autonomous control devices, but they are not intelligent agents. Regulating their design and operation is part of the general problem of ensuring the secure and beneficial use of technology.

In recent years, DNNs have been incorporated into autonomous control devices. They are now driving cars (at least experimentally), directing surgical robots, and performing a variety of other significant tasks. To the extent that an automatic system relies on a DNN for instructions and decision making, it becomes a locally, task-specific intelligent device. However, these systems are not agents with general intelligence of the kind postulated by singularity theorists. They resemble chess/Go playing models operating robotic mechanisms. They lack volition, freely chosen objectives, and domain general reasoning capacity. As we see from the current navigational difficulties associated with self-driving cars, the safety challenges that these systems pose are very much of the same kind that autonomous control technology has generated throughout its history.

NOTES

1 See *Moore's Law* on the Intel website at https://www.intel.com/content/www/ us/en/newsroom/resources/moores-law.html#:~:text=Moore's%20Law%20 is%20the%20observation,original%20paper%20published%20in%201965 for details of the law and the graph that it generates.

2 Chalmers (1996) takes consciousness as experienced through subjective mental states to be emergent. He argues that it cannot be reduced directly to neural activity in the brain or to any other set of physical events. Therefore, he embraces a variety of cognitive dualism. While this is an interesting and compelling view, it does not bear directly on the problem of superintelligence in AI, as I am characterising it here. Computational devices could achieve superrationality without having anything resembling an inner mental life of the kind that humans experience.

3 They also cite recent experimental neurolinguistic results, suggesting that linguistic knowledge and real-world reasoning are encoded in distinct parts of the brain.

4 See Dubhashi and Lappin (2017) for earlier versions of some of these arguments against the singularity.

5 See Bissell (2009) for an overview of the history of automatic control technology and the development of theoretical models of control.

CHAPTER 5

Risks Actual

5.1 RAPID EXPANSION OF TRANSFORMER MODEL SIZE

If the arguments presented in Chapter 4 are correct, then the rise of superintelligent artificial agents is not a pressing threat that we need to prioritise now. It may appear at some point in the future, but this does not seem likely or imminent. However, there is no shortage of serious problems that current and emerging AI technology does pose. It is important to characterise these clearly, in order to formulate effective responses to them. In this chapter, I will consider some of the more dangerous threats that AI is creating. This is by no means intended to be an exhaustive list. It is a set of examples that illustrate several of the more urgent risks connected with AI.

The rapid growth in the size of transformers, and the LLMs that they drive, is the source of at least two types of difficulty, which I will take up in Sections 5.2 and 5.3. The size of a transformer model M depends on three main factors:

1. The number of layers and attention head blocks in M

2. The number of parameters in M

3. The size of the data set on which M is pre-trained

Most of the expansion in the size of transformers has been in 2 and 3.

To get a sense of how sharp and rapid the growth in the number of parameters for LLMs has been, consider the transition from OpenAI's ChatGPT-2 through to ChatGPT-4 in the period from 2019 to 2023. The

DOI: 10.1201/9781003624790-5

numbers cited here are for the larger versions of these models. ChatGPT-2 has 1.5 billion parameters (Solaiman et al., 2019). ChatGPT-3 has 175 billion parameters (Brown et al., 2020). ChatGPT-4 has been estimated to have 1.76 trillion parameters (Lubbad, 2023).

A similar trajectory holds for the increase in pre-training data for ChatGPT (and other) models. ChatGPT-3 was pre-trained on 300 billion tokens of text (Brown et al., 2020). ChatGPT-4 is multi-modal, and so it is pre-trained on mixed visual and textual embeddings, as well as on word embeddings from text. OpenAI has not released details of the training and design of ChatGPT-4, but its multi-modal embeddings require significantly larger training sets than those of a transformer trained only on text. ChatGPT-4o is a recent update of ChatGPT-4, which fully integrates text, sound, and images. It is reasonable to assume that it required additional data for pre-training.

Narayanan et al. (2021) observe that ChatGPT-3 could be trained on 1024 A100 graphics processing units (GPUs) in just over a month. Minde (2023) estimates that Chat-GPT-4 required 25,000 Nvidia 100 GPUs for training. The cost of training ChatGPT-3 on a GPU cluster is estimated at $4 million (Li, 2020). Sam Altman of OpenAI is quoted as claiming that the cost of training ChatGPT-4 was $100 million (Knight, 2023).

In general, the accuracy and efficiency of a transformer improves in relation to its size, as measured in the number of parameters for the model, and the size of its pre-training and fine-tuning data. This is driving tech companies to produce ever larger large language models (LLMs), more rapidly. As a result, the problems discussed in the following subsections, particularly those described in the next two subsections, are becoming increasingly acute.

5.2 ENVIRONMENTAL PROBLEMS

The increase in transformer size is causing a variety of significant environmental problems. Saul and Bass (Bloomberg, March 9, 2023) claim that training ChatGPT-3 consumed 1.287 gigawatt hours (GWh) of electricity, which is equivalent to the annual usage of 120 American households. Minde suggests that training ChatGPT-4 consumed 50 GWh of electrical power, a massive increase. The large tech companies claim that they receive most of their energy from renewable sources. However, Halper and O'Donovan (2024) report that these companies are taking up much of the available green energy, forcing power companies to expand their use of fossil fuel plants to meet demand from other sources.

The problem is not limited to training and running LLMs. Lev-Ram (2024) points out that the manufacture of microchips (including GPUs) involves toxic chemicals, vast amounts of water, and large quantities of electricity. Citing Schneider Electric, she states that a chip production factory can consume up to 100 megawatts an hour. Relying on Intel data, she points out that these plants can use more than 100 million gallons of water a day. They produce thousands of tons of chemical waste annually, which must be disposed of. In addition to model training and chip production, AI companies require large data centres and server farms to run their products. These too consume substantial amounts of power and water.

In popular discussions of the climate change crisis in the press, large-scale carbon emissions and toxic chemical waste tend to be associated with transportation (cars and planes) and agriculture (particularly cattle). The extent to which the development and application of AI models in the commercial sector also cause major environmental damage is not always appreciated. It is necessary to address this issue as part of managing climate change and pollution. It should be regarded as integral to the effort to render AI safe and beneficial.

5.3 TECH COMPANY MONOPOLY ON RESEARCH

The second set of problems created by the rapid increase in transformer model size concerns the role of large tech companies in shaping research and development in AI. In Chapter 1, I pointed out that, according to the Stanford *Artificial Intelligence Index Report* for 2023, in 2022 these companies designed 32 leading machine learning models, while academic institutions created only three. This reflects a shift from universities to industry as the main venue for innovation in AI. It has become the dominant pattern in AI research. Given the size of transformer models, it is primarily large private technology companies that have the financial and computing resources to train and operate transformers. Researchers in universities, public scientific agencies, and small start-ups generally lack the means to design, train, and support LLMs.

As these models are the leading edge of current AI work, the large tech companies enjoy an effective monopoly of research on deep learning. Students and researchers in educational institutions and smaller agencies have increasingly become clients of the tech companies, in that much of their work consists in fine-tuning and testing transformers on alternative applications or tweaking aspects of their design. The main code and the architecture of the models tend to come from one of the companies.

As a consequence of this development, a major part of AI is directed at issues that advance the commercial interests of the tech companies. The focus on chatbot LLMs is a good example of this. These systems are producing lucrative returns on the investments of OpenAI, Microsoft, Meta, Google, and other companies. Much of this work is of high quality. However, significant engineering and foundational issues in AI are being neglected, apparently because they cannot be straightforwardly monetised. One of these issues is the development of significantly smaller deep learning models with radically different architecture. To be competitive with LLMs, such a system would have to infer patterns reliably from much less data. This would require smarter learning designs than those of current models, which rely on exposure to vast quantities of data, over extended training epochs, to achieve robust accuracy.

The foundational cognitive concerns that motivated much of the early work in AI are also receiving diminished attention. One of these concerns is exploring the respects in which AI learning systems resemble human learning and how they diverge from it. A second and related question is whether an efficient AI learner could acquire knowledge of natural language on the basis of the same data to which human language learners are exposed, according to a similar sequence of development. Yet a third concern is the extent to which the most successful deep neural networks (DNNs) bear genuine analogies to human brains in the way that each processes information. These are important scientific problems, but the answers to them are not likely to have immediate commercial application.

It is worth noting that not all scientific disciplines operate in this way. Particle physics receives extensive public support. The Large Hadron Collider was built by the member governments of the European Organisation for Nuclear Research (CERN) between 1998 and 2008, at a cost of ~$4.75 billion. CERN continues to fund its research projects, such as the discovery of the Higgs boson particle, announced in 2012. Tech companies also support important basic research and engineering in particle physics, particularly in connection with semiconductors, and quantum computing. But the progress that has been made in this field would not have been possible without large-scale public investment in costly equipment and experiments that government agencies like CERN provide.

By contrast, with the emergence of the deep learning revolution, AI has become increasingly dominated by commercial engineering applications. Large tech companies now play a controlling role in determining the scientific research agenda and the nature of the models that are developed to advance this agenda. This focus has certainly produced interesting and important work. It has also marginalised a wide range of potentially fruitful research programs in both basic science and in engineering.

5.4 DISINFORMATION AND DEEP FAKES

As we have seen in Chapters 2 and 3, the deep learning revolution has produced powerful devices for generating natural language speech and text, visual images, music and audio effects, and videos. The current state of the art for generative AI models is such that many of their constructions are indistinguishable from human creations. The use of this technology to fabricate deep fakes of photographs, speech, and artistic performances has created a flood of online content that harms the well-being of the people who are being victimised by it. Manufactured pornography is circulated to hurt women. Public figures are misrepresented. Documents are forged, and digital identities are stolen. Criminal groups and hostile governments circulate an avalanche of false information to manipulate entire populations for financial or political gain.

Deep fakes and false news have already ravaged the internet and done large-scale social damage over the past few years. They have intensified division in public debate, misled voters in elections, and accentuated social conflict. They have undermined public faith in mainstream media and a range of political institutions. As generative models become increasingly sophisticated their capacity for large-scale damage will continue to increase. Imagine the possible impact of results reported for fabricated clinical experiments in fake scientific journals that look to be entirely genuine. They could create pervasive distrust in proper medical advice and legitimate medications. False reporting in simulated versions of reputable financial news services could cause panic in markets and disrupt economies. In short, we could soon find ourselves living in an environment where separating fact from malicious fiction becomes increasingly difficult. At that point the shared beliefs needed to sustain cohesion within the public domain begin to give way to doubt, recrimination, and chaos. The conditions for organised social activity and communication become unstuck.

What measures, if any, can we take to prevent this vortex of collapse? Developing effective systems for verifying online content is crucial to combatting disinformation.[1] If we can identify reliable information, then we can filter out questionable content and disinformation as the complement set. I will briefly consider three candidate procedures for online content verification. First, let's look at RAG (retrieval-augmented generation), which I introduced in Section 3.1 in connection with Q&A systems. RAG is a method for updating an LLM through fine-tuning on current data available from online sources. We introduced it as a possible way of preventing a generative transformer from hallucinating. Hallucination is a close relative of deep fake and other forms of disinformation. Unfortunately, as we noticed when discussing RAG as a solution to this earlier problem, it is not reliable as a verification method. There is no guarantee that the content which it accesses for update purposes is reliable.

A second approach, which Gambín et al. (2024) suggest, is to use a distributed ledger network to control online information (Soltani et al., 2022). This is a network in which every transaction is copied to each node and verified across the entire network to insure reliability. The information transferred is encrypted. The block chains used for cryptocurrencies are an instance of a distributed ledger network. There are at least two serious problems with these networks. First, adding nodes greatly increases the complexity of computation required for transferring and recording information. Therefore, as the network grows, it requires sharply expanding amounts of time and resources. It consumes large amounts of energy, and it is environmentally harmful. The second and more obvious difficulty is that such a network is not a viable system for posting and accessing most content on the internet. Given its highly restrictive nature, it would not allow for many of the activities that now flow freely through the net. The security that it affords would be achieved at the cost of paralysing most of the news, communication, commerce, and much else that makes up normal online traffic.

The third option for content verification is digital watermarking (Hwang and Oh, 2023). This involves inserting a hidden digital code in text, images, or sound recordings. A variety of procedures have been developed for watermarking the outputs of generative AI models. Watermarks permit one to verify the source and authenticity of data. They can be counterfeited or removed. However, they do provide a partial solution to the problem of verifying online data. Watermarking offers one of the more workable procedures for ensuring the source of online content. Further work is required to render it robust, wide coverage, and reliable.

5.5 HATE SPEECH

The proliferation of racist and gender targeted abuse, as well as religious prejudice and anti-immigrant sentiment, is one of the most dangerous features of current social media. Many of the platforms hosting these media apply customisation algorithms to identify users' preferences and to modify their content feeds accordingly. If these procedures detect a tendency to bigotry, some of the platforms will direct the user to sites and groups that promote it. This will amplify hate speech and expand the online market for it. It also produces closed digital communities that are exposed only to one type of view, in this case a repugnant one. In addition to customisation algorithms, AI contributes to this pattern through chatbots that generate hate speech automatically, greatly increasing the volume of this material throughout the internet. The extensive spread of online hate speech is not merely a source of offensive digital content. It serves as an organising tool for racist groups and other extremist agencies that recruit activists and terrorists to their causes.

Until recently, the venues committed to combatting abusive posts relied primarily on human moderators. Given the flood of such content, this is not an efficient strategy. A considerable amount of research in NLP (natural language processing) and multi-modal processing is now devoted to using LLMs to detect hate speech.[2] This involves using transformers for discrimination and classification of text and images, rather than for generation. Developing a robust hate speech classifier is a complex task involving semantic interpretation and understanding of context. Keyword- and phrase-driven recognition will not yield accurate results. It will miss subtler forms of abuse in which non-offensive terms and images are used for malicious purposes. There is a considerable amount of coded bigotry that relies on euphemism and dog whistle expressions.

One of the main problems in broad coverage, cross-domain hate speech detection is the absence of large annotated training sets for fine-tuning transformers. Pendzel et al. (2023) propose to solve this difficulty by using ChatGPT-2 to generate a large synthetic corpus, annotated with both normal text and hate speech, from existing smaller hand-annotated corpora. They report a significant improvement in the performance of several BERT-type models in recall of hate speech, when they are fine-tuned on a hand-annotated corpus that is extended through synthetic data.

Gilardi et al. (2023) describe an experiment in which ChatGPT-3.5 is compared to human Amazon Mechanical Turk annotators on four distinct types of text classification task.[3] These are (i) determining relevance to a topic, (ii) identifying stance (opinion) on an issue, (iii) recognising the topic, and (iv) two frame problems. The gold standard for assessing both ChatGPT-3.5 and the crowdsource workers was a test set that two trained experts had annotated for these tasks. Gilardi et al. found that ChatGPT-3.5 significantly outperformed the MTurk annotators on all of the classification problems. It was not fine-tuned, but it was applied directly to the test set. The fact that it did so well on domain general text classification problems, with zero-shot learning, suggests that later versions of the model could achieve a high level of accuracy for hate speech detection across different domains.

Hate speech detection is an important tool in constraining digital abuse. It allows us to quickly identify the phenomenon automatically, over large amounts of text, in real time. However, it does not, in itself, solve the problem. The fact that we have effective automatic devices for recognising hate speech leaves open the questions of whether we can control it, and if so, how.[4] In the United States, First Amendment rights protect most types of abusive language. While many other countries have laws that ban several varieties of bigoted speech when they involve group defamation, applying them online is difficult. Most of the companies that host the social media platforms on which abuse is rampant operate from outside of the countries where these laws apply. In addition to free speech questions, there is also the problem of deciding on who is legally responsible for abusive digital content, the platform provider, or the people who post it. It is also not generally clear who is liable for any damage that hate speech may cause and which agency, if any, is responsible for regulating it. These are questions of public policy rather than AI engineering. They are of major social importance, and they warrant detailed consideration. I will return to them in Chapter 6.

5.6 BIAS IN DECISION-MAKING

In Chapter 3, I discussed several applications of AI systems that are transforming work, medical treatment, and art. Other important domains where AI technology is now prominent include policing and criminal justice, the finance and loan industry, and the labour market. AI systems are used to predict likely outcomes and to evaluate risk in these areas. They are being enlisted to recommend decisions and courses of action on the basis of these predictions.

Unfortunately, it is becoming increasingly apparent that many of the AI models that are used for these purposes suffer from bias against vulnerable groups characterised by their ethnic, religious, gender, socio-economic, age, geographic, or health properties, among others. So, for example, face recognition programs employed by police and security services tend to discriminate against people of colour. Software that predicts expected levels of academic achievement may work to the disadvantage of poorer people living in remote rural areas. Models that assess suitability for higher managerial roles often favour men over women. Programs that determine eligibility for insurance, and premium levels, often discriminate against immigrants, people of colour, and older people. Research on devising effective techniques for eliminating bias and ensuring equitability in AI guided decision-making is ongoing. It remains an open problem of the utmost importance.[5]

To get a sense of how bias enters an AI predictive model, and possible ways of combatting it, let's briefly look at three areas in which these models are applied. These are health care, hiring, and loans.

Nazer et al. (2023) observe that the way in which the large AI models that predict illness and prescribe treatments are trained on data distorts the distribution patterns for many health conditions. For example, sickle cell anaemia is far more common among people of African descent than white Europeans. But in Europe and North America, they are a minority of the population. Similarly, Tay-Sachs disease is significantly more likely to occur among Jews of Ashkenazi background than in other groups. A variety of conditions affect more women than men (and vice versa for others). Disease prediction models trained on large sets of randomly sampled data will not accurately reflect these probability differences. Therefore, the diagnoses that they give for particular cases and the treatments that they recommend may be inappropriate.

Overfitting to the training data is an obvious source of this problem. It consists in the model being too closely tied to the distribution patterns that it sees in its training data. This prevents it from generalising accurately to test sets from other data domains. Such a model would generate the wrong probability distribution for a population drawn from a different group than its training set. Given this skewed distribution, its assessments and recommendations may well be entirely unsuitable. As a result, the groups that are under-represented in the training data would be disadvantaged in the treatment that they receive, when it is informed by these AI systems.

One way of correcting for overfitting is to apply adversarial training. This involves adding problematic data points to the training set in order to force the model to modify the generalisations that it infers. A second method is to fine-tune the model on population-specific data when applying it to groups that are under-represented in the pre-training set. A third technique requires extensive out of domain testing to assess a model's accuracy for data that is substantially different than its training data. If its performance declines significantly for such test sets, then expert human feedback can be used to correct the model. These are standard procedures of machine learning to improve the robustness of predictive systems for comparatively non-typical cases. They are labour-intensive and expensive to apply. They also do not insure fully accurate and equitable medical AI models. Clearly far more research and engineering are needed to deal with this problem.

AI systems are widely employed in job recruitment and hiring. They rank CVs according to correlation with the requirements of a job ad. They analyse videos of candidate interviews on the basis of visual and audio features of a candidate's linguistic and social interaction patterns. They assess an applicant's skills through the descriptions that they provide of their training and their previous experience.

Biases are incorporated into the models that support these systems in precisely the way that we have observed with AI applications in medical care.[6] CV assessment and video evaluation systems that are pre-trained on data in which under-represented groups have a marginal presence will favour a majority population in their predictions and recommendations. If this overfitting is not corrected, it will result in unfair exclusion of a range of minority and women candidates. Techniques like adversarial training, fine-tuning, and human monitoring with intervention will go some way to repairing the biases that distort AI job applicant assessment programs. Much work is still needed to discover the different sorts of prejudices inherent in these systems and to devise effective methods for eliminating them.

Finally, AI procedures are now pervasive in assessing credit rating and deciding on loan applications.[7] Zou and Khern-am-nuai (2023) report a revealing set of experiments that identify the source of ethnic bias in mortgage approvals. They train a statistical model on data for loan applications from the US housing market. They demonstrate that the data set encodes statistically significant discrimination against African American applicants, compared to members of other ethnicities, who are combined into a single control group. This bias is not simply a matter of correlation between racial self-identification and rate of loan approval. It is revealed as a strong prejudice, through the pairing of Black and control group applicants with similar income and credit profiles. The disparity in loans granted remains substantial when these profile variables are correlated. Zou and Khern-am-nuai then train a predictive statistical model on this database. Interestingly, it not only preserves the bias but amplifies it by increasing the difference in loan recommendations for the control group vs African Americans.

They also test a model that filters out the bias, yielding the same rate of mortgage approvals and amounts for both groups. However, this system is acutely problematic. It is considerably less accurate than the biased model. A higher percentage of its recommendations are false positives in that they suggest granting mortgages to applicants who are not credit worthy. Such a defect would incur considerable cost for a mortgage company that used it. These modelling experiments illustrate clearly both the seriousness of the problem of bias in using AI models trained on existing data, in many domains, and the difficulties involved in re-engineering them to eliminate the bias in a manageable way.

5.7 JOB DISPLACEMENT AND SHARP INCOME INEQUALITY

Dubhashi and Lappin (2017) cite Brynjolfsson and McAfee's (2014) study of the economic effects of digital technology to argue that AI could create large-scale unemployment across a wide range of professions. They observe that, unlike previous industrial revolutions, AI has general application to many different tasks. Therefore, job loss will be more widespread, and the new industries that technological change creates will also be subject to automation. In earlier cases when a new technology emerged, the jobs that were lost were recouped through the new industries that it powered. The unemployment that accompanied the replacement of horse-drawn vehicles by trains and cars was balanced out by new professions in the rail and motor industries. Such compensatory job creation is not an obvious consequence of the rise of AI. It will not be limited to displacement in a specific trade. Instead, it is exposing work to automation throughout the labour market, at most levels of skill, across many domains.

Another important result of the rise of AI is that the distribution of income and wealth is increasingly skewed to an elite of tech entrepreneurs who develop, market, and support AI systems, as well as to the scientists and engineers who they employ. These companies are now powerful actors in the economy and in the political domain. They are able to shape regulatory legislation to suit their interests and to minimise their tax burdens. They also play a major role in shaping public opinion through the social media venues that they host and control.

More recent work on the impact of AI on the job market (Jung and Desikan, 2023; OECD, 2023; Green, 2024) confirms that a large spectrum of skilled non-manual professions are now highly exposed to automation. These include, among others, tax advisors, clerical workers, legal secretaries, medical diagnosticians, translators, editors, and copy writers. As we saw in Chapter 3, current AI systems are transforming the methods with which work in these, and numerous other domains, is performed. As the integration of AI into robotics develops, it is also reasonable to expect displacement in skilled manufacturing, and many service positions.

As this trend accelerates, it may instantiate the dangers that Dubhashi and Lappin (and many others) have been warning of. Large-scale job displacement, together with an increasing concentration of wealth in the hands of large tech companies, could create significant social disruption and political conflict. To avoid this scenario, it will be necessary to implement measures that create new employment horizons and to provide support for those who suffer displacement. It will also be necessary to find effective ways in which to regulate both the economic and the political power of tech companies. Private companies exist to maximise profit. They are not likely to ensure (near) full employment or redistribute wealth on their own. Nor can they be expected to constrain their political influence voluntarily. These objectives are social benefits that would limit rather than enhance corporate profits. How best to achieve them is a major public policy issue. I will discuss it briefly in Chapter 6.

NOTES

1 See Shoaib et al. (2023) and Loth et al. (2024) for surveys of the role of AI in producing disinformation and possible ways in which AI systems can be used to counteract it.

2 Kumarage et al. (2024) offer an overview of some of this work.

3 Mechanical Turk is an Amazon service for recruiting anonymous crowd-source workers to perform online tasks that produce data for computer science and cognitive science experiments.

4 Parker and Ruths (2023) discuss some of these questions.

5 See Ferrara (2024) for a survey of bias in AI decision-making and recent work on mitigating this bias.

6 Albaroudi et al. (2024) discuss the ways in which bias enters into AI-guided hiring decisions. They also look at AI procedures for filtering out these biases.

7 Garcia et al. (2024) present a detailed literature survey of research on algorithmic bias in the financial industry.

CHAPTER 6

Towards a Rational Public Policy on AI

6.1 LARGE TECH COMPANIES AS QUASI-MONOPOLIES

In Chapter 5, I discussed the way in which large tech companies, like OpenAI, Google, Meta, Apple, and Microsoft, have come to monopolise the design and development of transformers and the large language models (LLMs) that they support. This is due to the large-scale of computing resources, data, and energy that are required to train and operate these systems. I mentioned the fact, noted in the Stanford *Artificial Intelligence Index Report* for 2023, that in 2022 tech companies created 32 major machine learning models. By contrast, universities produced three. The concentration of engineering power in the hands of the tech companies is allowing them to exercise control over the direction of research in AI and to shape the formulation of the scientific questions that drive the field.

I also noted that this is not the case in all areas of scientific research. Particle physics, for example, relies primarily on massive public support for the very expensive equipment required for its experimental work. In order to balance the impact of private tech companies on AI, it is necessary to significantly increase government spending on AI within universities, smaller research agencies, and start-up companies pursuing promising directions that are not receiving private investment.

DOI: 10.1201/9781003624790-6

Research is not the only area where the tech companies play a monopolistic role. Khan (2017) is a (now classic) study of the way in which Amazon has come to control a variety of markets, forcing out competition. These include online consumer purchasing, entertainment streaming, e-publishing, shipping and delivery services, and crowdsourcing. Khan observes that Amazon employs long-term predatory pricing (charging below cost) and vertical control of multiple states of a business process, to achieve a pervasive market presence throughout different parts of the e-commerce market. She also points out that it uses the extensive data that it extracts from its client businesses to compete with them.

Original US anti-trust legislation formulated in the first part of the twentieth century to deal with monopolistic businesses like railroads, banks, and oil companies, in the gilded robber baron age, was aimed at constraining both predatory pricing and vertical expansion of control over the production and supply process. But this legislation was reconstructed in the latter half of the previous century to focus on consumer welfare. It sought to protect consumers by preventing excessive pricing due to an absence of competition. Therefore, it is not suited to dealing with cases like Amazon, in which below cost pricing is pursued over a long period of time, in order to secure market expansion, with investors prepared to sustain the losses involved in this strategy. As a quasi-monopolistic position is achieved, the revenue stream rises sharply.

Khan concludes that returning to the principles of the original anti-trust legislation of the progressive era in the United States would be one effective way of dealing with overbearing market control of the kind that Amazon now exercises. She became the chair of the US Federal Trade Commission under President Biden, where she pursued this approach in dealing with the tech companies. She has recently been replaced by the Trump administration.

Other US agencies have sought to apply existing anti-trust laws to tech companies. The Department of Justice brought a successful suit against Microsoft in 1998 for arranging with other tech companies to include its web browser, Explorer, in their products. The original decision on the suit called for Microsoft to be broken up into constituent companies, as Bell telephone had been in the 1980s. This and many other provisions of the decision against Microsoft were overturned on appeal and in a settlement with the Bush administration in 2001. More recently, a federal district judge ruled that Google operates as a monopoly in the way in which its search engine is incorporated into a variety of online systems.[1] The

European Union has also brought several anti-trust suits against a number of tech companies.[2]

In fact, the influence of tech companies extends well beyond e-commerce and search engines. They provide the platforms for social media, and so they control the venues within which much news is exchanged and public attitudes are formed. Government offices, financial institutions, schools, universities, transportation agencies, and many other organisations increasingly rely on them for the online services that they provide. These are often contracted out to the tech companies, with data processed and stored on their servers. AI is becoming prominent in the provision of these services, through, *inter alia*, voice recognition, speech and text generation, dialogue management, information retrieval, and question answering.[3]

It is not at all obvious that anti-trust legislation, regardless of how it is formulated, will be sufficient to constrain many of the destructive effects of large tech and the AI systems that they are now deploying. It is more likely that extensive public regulatory regimes will be required to reign in these enterprises. I will take up some of the problems that seem to invite such regulation in the following sections.

Because of the enormous wealth that tech companies have now accumulated, they wield considerable political influence. They have frequently deployed it to lobby against regulation of their activities. They have employed a variety of arguments to support the claim that they should not be subject to binding government oversight. One of the most prominent is that regulation will stifle their capacity to innovate. A second is that they are responsible enterprises that are able and willing to govern themselves in the public interest without the need for external intervention.

Neither of these arguments is particularly persuasive, and both are completely self-serving. First, all other major industries are regulated, and this has not undermined their ability to innovate. The transportation and the pharmaceutical industries must satisfy rigorous safety conditions. Advertising and public relations are subject to truth in advertising laws. The food industry has health and safety requirements. All have achieved profitability through continuing change and renewal. Second, no business voluntarily operates in the public interest as its primary concern. It exists to make money, and it would cease to function if it was not profitable over a long period of time. It obeys rigorous safety and labour conditions only because it is legally compelled to do so. Overseeing consumer and worker safety, as well as ensuring equitable treatment in the market place, is one of the main functions of the public domain in a democracy. These concerns apply with equal force to the tech companies that create, market, and apply AI systems.

6.2 CONSTRAINING DISINFORMATION

In Section 5.4, I considered possible ways of counteracting deep fakes produced by generative AI models. I suggested that watermarking may offer a partial solution to the problem of verifying the authenticity of the source of digital content. However, watermarking does not solve the general problem of disinformation that is spread across the internet, often amplified by AI chatbots and other content creators. Verifying the source of disinformation will not, in itself, stop the distribution and the influence of maliciously false content.

Distortions and misrepresentations of the facts can have highly damaging consequences. Two clear examples of the harm that disinformation causes are the violent attack on the US Capitol on 6 January 2021, in response to false reports that the presidential election had been "stolen", and resistance to COVID vaccines due to unfounded claims about their adverse effect on one's health. Much of the material that generated these two developments appeared on Facebook and other social media networks which it owns (currently under Meta), such as Instagram and WhatsApp. Facebook had, until recently, what it presents as a stringent policy of removing harmful content from its sites and of using fact-checking moderation to reduce inaccurate posts. Silverman et al. (2022) show that this program was ineffective in controlling the flood of "stop the steal" sites and the incitement that accompanied them in the lead up to the January 6 Capitol riot.

Broniatowski et al. (2023) provide a detailed study of Facebook's handling of anti-vaxer disinformation during the COVID pandemic. Their results indicate that while the company did indeed remove many anti-vaxer posts and sites, the structure of its network allowed continued extensive access to disinformation on vaccines after this content was pruned. They suggest that the level of user engagement with anti-vaxer material did not diminish after removal, but it simply moved through other channels and links. Moreover, the intensity of the disinformation actually increased. Both cases cast serious doubt on the view that the companies that host sites where disinformation is rife are able, or even willing, to restrict it through self-regulation and internal moderation.

Imposing government legislation on internet platforms to control disinformation is controversial, both as a matter of principle and with respect to its effectiveness. The American model, based on First Amendment constitutional protection of unrestricted free speech, provides one extreme in the spectrum of legislative approaches. It allows all content that does not violate existing federal and state laws on incitement to violence, child pornography, and other forms of expressly specified criminal activity. Kirtley (2018) offers a defence of this approach in the context of the debate over the rise of "fake news" on the internet. She cites the landmark Supreme Court ruling on the case of *The New York Times* v. Sullivan (1964) to argue for the constitutional right to be wrong in the claims that one makes publicly. This ruling requires that to be successful in a libel or defamation suite the plaintiff demonstrate not only that the published assertions are false and damage his/her reputation, but that they were advanced with malicious intent. This restriction on defamation distinguishes US libel law from the more permissive British law, where falsity and damage to reputation have, in the past, been sufficient to support a court action. By extension publishing disinformation on social media platforms is not, in itself, illegal in most cases, regardless of the harm that it may cause.

One of the primary motivations for this libertarian perspective is that the unrestricted free expression of opinion ("the free market of ideas") is the most efficient way of discovering the truth through the competition of views in the public domain. Admirable as this doctrine might be in principle, it encounters at least two serious problems in practice. First, free speech protections have been formulated, for the most part, to defend the right to express unpopular ideas in the face of government repression. But the tech companies have achieved a virtual monopoly on digital platforms for social media and digital publication. They control the expression of opinion and the flow of information in these venues. It is through their channels that consumers are exposed to large quantities of false and harmful information, which host companies have shown themselves unable to filter effectively. They resemble the monopolistic newspaper chains of the first part of the twentieth century. Anti-trust laws were introduced in part to restrain their power in the news industry. However, in the current situation, breaking up the tech companies may well not be economically feasible. It would also not be an effective way of halting the continuing rise of disinformation in the digital domain. Regulation appears to offer the only way of constraining it.

Second, even within the American context speech is not entirely unrestricted. Truth in advertising laws provide for serious legal and financial sanctions against companies and individuals that publish false or misleading claims for products or services that they are marketing.[4] These laws are designed to protect consumers against predatory advertising from unscrupulous commercial agents. Moreover, the publishers who provide venues for false ads are not exempt from liability for their content, even if they did not produce it. In addition, the US criminal code (18 U.S. Code Section 2101) outlaws incitement to riot. It identifies incitement to insurrection as a crime (18 U.S. Code Section 2383). These legal measures are intended to restrict speech that causes major social harm either to consumers in a market, or to the peace and safety of people in their daily lives. It is not at all obvious that spreading false information intended to disrupt a democratic election, or to undermine faith in crucial public health measures during a pandemic, is less damaging to the public good than the kind of speech that US law currently proscribes.

In addition to the American model, there are several alternative legal approaches to dealing with disinformation on the internet. Shattock (2021) considers EU legislation, such as the Disinformation in Digital Services Act, which the European Parliament approved in 2022. He points out that a problem with this and other EU codes of practice for the tech companies is that they tend to be fairly weak, given the existence of a multiplicity of distinct regulatory regimes in the countries of the European Union. Tan (2022) compares the digital regulations of Singapore, Australia, and Germany. Singapore has enacted a reasonably comprehensive set of measures, but it is difficult to use them to constrain disinformation, given that most of the content originates from outside of the country. Australia has a far narrower set of restrictions, which are of limited use in dealing with the problem. Germany imposes substantial financial penalties on companies that fail to remove content identified as dangerous, but monitoring and implementation are only partially effective.

Distinguishing between the legitimate expression of false or misguided opinions that should be protected in a free society, and spreading harmful disinformation of the kind that merits legal intervention, is a complex and difficult exercise in legal reasoning and legislative design. This does not exempt us from dealing with this problem. It is one of the main challenges of formulating reasonable public policy for regulating the tech companies that support both AI and the major social media platforms in which it is increasingly applied. It clearly requires an international solution, as individual countries are not in a position to deal with multinational companies that host content from outside of their territories. International trade agreements may provide one of the devices that can be used to impose effective regulation on the tech companies.

6.3 INTELLECTUAL PROPERTY RIGHTS

In Chapter 3, I described a range of applications in which AI systems are revolutionising the environments in which we live and work. These applications are creating a number of serious problems concerning intellectual property (IP) rights. They fall into two major categories. The first involves the data on which AI models are trained. The second concerns ownership of the content that these models generate. Existing IP legislation does not cover either in a straightforward way. A variety of court cases in different countries have been launched to attempt to settle some of these issues. Legislative proposals have been advanced in the United States, the European Union, and other parts of the world in an attempt to regulate the use of both types of AI activity. There is an extensive literature on the IP problems that current AI applications pose.[5]

As we have seen in previous chapters, LLMs are trained on very large quantities of data. This consists of online texts, digital images, videos, and sound recordings. Much of this material is copyrighted by its creators. These include literary works, scientific papers, newspaper articles, photographs, reproductions of paintings, musical recordings, films, and a host of other assets. For the most part, tech companies have not requested the permission of content creators when training on their data. In some of the legal actions that writers, artists, and publishers have brought against this practice, the companies have used *fair use* as a defence. Fair use allows reproduction of texts and images for purposes of critical discussion and education. It also permits what is known as *transformative use* of copyrighted material, where this involves applying the content in an entirely innovative way, not originally envisaged by the original creators. Some of the tech companies claim that training an AI system on copyrighted data is an instance of a transformative use of these assets.

Rajan (2024) discusses the recent suit that *The New York Times* brought against OpenAI and Microsoft for use of its articles in training their respective models. The companies invoked the transformative version of a fair use defence in that case. They argued that the LLMs that they have trained use the copyrighted data in an entirely novel way, unrelated to the original purposes of its creators. She also cites the fact that Google invoked this argument in responding to suits on its partial republication of copyrighted books. Google ultimately won its case, but *The New York*

Times vs OpenAI and Microsoft suit remains ongoing. Fair use defences of copyrighted digital material are uncertain and controversial. Rajan mentions the Goldsmith vs Warhol decision of 2023, in which the US Supreme Court found the Andy Warhol Foundation liable for the unlicensed use of Linda Goldsmith's 1981 photograph of Prince. Warhol's silk screen images of Prince were based on Goldstein's photograph, and they appeared in a 2016 issue of *Vanity Fair* devoted to the musician.

Regardless of whether the fair use defence for LLM training is ultimately upheld in American courts, it is clear that training data adds considerable value to the products that the tech companies produce and market. Therefore, it seems entirely unreasonable that they should enjoy free access to this material without requiring the consent of the content creators, and not paying them any compensation for its use. At a minimum, these companies should be required to receive the consent of the copyright holders for the protected data that they use. In the interests of transparency, they should also be obliged to list the materials on which their systems are trained and to indicate that permission was granted. Finally, profit sharing in the form of licensing fees or royalties paid to the content creators is strongly motivated. This is the way that music streaming companies compensate artists whose compositions they market.

What about the content that AI systems produce? There are two main questions to consider. First, how original is this content? Second, who owns it? Concerning the first, if the AI creation is highly derivative of its training data, then the same problem of compensating the original creators for their data arises. Again, permission to use, acknowledgement of training sources, and, possibly, financial compensation are all relevant in this context. Resolving these questions is a complex task. It will depend heavily on the extent to which the generated material clearly resembles the model's training sources.

On the second question, ownership is a particularly interesting problem. Picht et al. (2023) consider the arguments for and against recognising AI systems as candidates for patent and copyright assignment. To give them this status is to grant them significant legal rights. The motivation for doing so is, presumably, that they created the content for which they are recognised as the patent/copyright holder. The problem with such a move is that it bestows rights on artefacts. Non-human animals enjoy legal protections by virtue of the fact that they are sentient. They suffer pain, and they can enjoy pleasure. These protections are intended to promote their welfare. AI systems, like other constructed devices, are not sentient, nor are they intelligent agents in the sense that I specify in Chapter 4. It is not clear what benefits they could enjoy if given ownership of their creations. Nor is it obvious what injustice or deprivation they would suffer if they are not accorded rights of ownership. What use would they have for any income that might accrue from fees or royalties on their content? It would be, at best, odd to regard it as an injustice not to pay them wages for the labour that they perform. If they cannot be salaried workers, then on what grounds could we admit them to the free professions? Hence, licensing fees and royalties are also not relevant for these devices. It follows that they are not possible owners of their content in any legally interesting sense.

If, in fact, AI systems are not candidates for proprietorship of their creations, then the obvious alternatives are the tech companies that build and market these systems, and the human clients who use them for content production. Resolving which of these two has the claim to ownership in each case is difficult. It will require both extensive legal argument and reflection on what arrangement best promotes social benefit. Different decisions will invariably be required for distinct types of cases.

Finally, it is worth observing that while most discussions of IP and AI have focussed on generative AI models that create new content, discriminative AI models, like those taken up in Chapter 3, also pose important questions in this area. Applying a model to identify an abnormality in an X-ray, to authenticate a painting, or to classify the genre and authorship of a musical composition requires extensive training of the same kind that goes into developing a generative LLM. Recognition, authentication, and classification also have commercial applications. Therefore, issues of copyright and fair compensation for content are not unique to generative models. They both apply with equal force to discriminative and classificatory AI systems.

6.4 REGULATING HATE SPEECH

In Section 5.5, I briefly reviewed current research on AI procedures for detecting online hate speech, and I observed that some of the work is yielding increasingly effective tools for identifying this phenomenon. The issues involved in regulating hate speech are closely related to those that arise in constraining disinformation. The leading approaches to this problem run parallel to those proposed for handing disinformation.

American First Amendment rights protect most hate speech, as they do the bulk of online disinformation. The arguments that are advanced to defend this view are essentially the same as those that motivate the protection of other types of offensive speech and publication. Unrestricted speech is characterised as a basic human right in a democracy, and the antidote to pernicious comment is free counterargument. Because most tech companies that provide social media platforms are based in the United States, this makes legal regulation of hate speech difficult. As in the case of digital disinformation, the tech companies have a virtual monopoly on the social media platforms through which hate speech is disseminated and amplified. Countering it effectively through free argument in the "marketplace of ideas" is entirely unrealistic, given the resources that are available for its promotion. To describe such content as offensive, but efficiently dealt with by reply in open debate, seriously trivialises the damage that it produces through incitement to violence, abuse, and discrimination. The image of a town hall meeting that extreme libertarians invoke to characterise the give and take of free argument bears no resemblance to a digital space increasingly dominated by armies of trolls and bots disseminating toxic propaganda, against which targeted individuals and groups have little, if any, defence.

It is worth noting that American civil libertarian acceptance of racist and other forms of hate speech is very much an outlier even in the North American context. The Canadian Federal Criminal Code contains three statutes banning certain types of defamation, passed by Parliament in 1970. Section 318 outlaws calls for genocide. Section 319(1) makes the public incitement of hatred a criminal offence punishable by up to two years in prison. According to Section 319(2), wilfully promoting hatred against an identifiable group carries the same penalty.

At the opposite end of the spectrum, Singapore adopted the Protection from Online Falsehoods and Manipulation Act (POFMA) in 2019. It places stringent restrictions on the publication of false information and of hate content. Between these opposing regulatory approaches, the European Union and individual European countries (including the United Kingdom) have legislation of varying degrees of severity, restricting racist and bigoted incitement.[6]

All of these measures encounter at least three types of difficulty. The first is characterising hate speech in a way that is sufficiently substantive to capture racism, sexism, and similar sorts of abuse, while still permitting free expression of opinion, even when it is obnoxious, but not threatening. The second problem is devising effective mechanisms of enforcement. As we have seen, self-moderation by the tech companies is not particularly effective, given the commercial interest that they have in maximising traffic on their own media sites. Individual countries have limited capacity to control the flow of abusive content because of the international nature of the digital platforms that host it. Finally, most anti-hate speech measures do not hold the platform providers legally responsible for the content that they publish. In this respect, the providers are treated very differently than traditional publishers and broadcast media.

A rational public policy on regulating online hate speech must resolve these three issues. Striking a reasonable balance between filtering out digital abuse while sustaining robust freedom of expressions is an ongoing difficulty. It will only emerge over time through continuing discussion, experimentation with alternative policies, test cases, and the accumulation of legal precedents. Enforcement remains an acute difficulty. Neither national anti-hate legislation nor international human rights law seems to provide a fully effective means for controlling digital hate content. International trade agreements might offer a supplementary mechanism for imposing constraints on tech companies hosting social media platforms. If respecting anti-hate requirements becomes a legally binding condition for doing business in a lucrative market, then social media platforms will not be able to avoid these constraints. Such agreements could also shift at least some of the responsibility for digital content published on these platforms to the hosts, treating them as publishers, rather than as passive venues. Clearly, how best to regulate online hate will remain a complex open problem for the foreseeable future.

6.5 AVOIDING BIAS

In Section 5.6, I considered several domains in which AI systems are used to assess candidates and recommend decisions. These include, among others, law enforcement, medical treatment, credit rating, and loan approval. There is ample evidence that the models that support these systems frequently incorporate significant biases relating to ethnicity, gender, age, social class, and geographic location. Attempts to eliminate these biases through refined machine learning procedures have yielded mixed results, occasionally creating new difficulties.

There are at least two closely related questions that a reasonable public policy on eliminating bias in the application of AI models must contend with. The first problem is who bears responsibility for these decisions, the designers of the system, or the agency that employs it. The second is should we attempt to regulate the AI systems, or just the results of their decision-making.

Concerning the first issue, the designers of a biased AI system could argue that it is the users who train it and apply its decisions. Therefore, the user is legally responsible for any discrimination that an individual, or a group, suffers through its application. The user can reply that they are relying on the expertise of the software designer to provide a reliable, bias-free device for evaluating people and recommending the preferred course of action. Therefore, the producer of the product is responsible for any damage that it causes, if it is applied according to the designer's instructions. Both positions have merit. Whichever way this question is resolved, clear and effective measures need to be devised to protect the people who are directly affected by expert AI models. These will be natural extensions of existing anti-discrimination legislation, which is a central element of any enlightened legal system.

Clearly, the answer we embrace for the second question follows directly from the approach that we adopt to the first. If users are solely or primarily responsible for any discriminatory decisions that an AI system generates, then they bear legal liability for this damage under anti-discrimination law. It is not necessary to regulate AI expert systems, but only the results of applying them. However, if the creator of the system is held accountable for the damage that it causes through biased decision-making, then we are seeking to eliminate discrimination from the architecture of the model and its training procedures. This requires an additional level of regulation.

There are problems of both principle and efficiency in resolving these questions. In the end, it will be necessary to determine what is the most effective way of ensuring that people are treated equitably when subjected to assessment and decision-making with an AI model. It appears that recourse to human monitoring, and, in at least some cases, intervention at crucial points in the operation of these systems, is a necessary condition for filtering out their biases. This requires that expert systems be applied only in collaboration with expert human agents, who check the data on which they are trained and who diligently vet their recommendations.

6.6 DEALING WITH THE ECONOMIC EFFECTS OF AI

I briefly discussed the possible economic impact of the AI revolution in Section 5.7. The prospect of widespread job loss through the increasing pace of automation across a wide range of professions poses the most serious concern in this area. In previous technological transformations, the disappearance of traditional types of employment in one industry was offset by the creation of labour-intensive manufacturing and service jobs in newly emerging areas of the economy. Transitions were difficult for the displaced part of the labour force, but increased prosperity was eventually achieved.

AI-driven automation threatens a different sort of displacement. It could render many positions obsolete across much of the economy, within a comparatively short period of time. This process could affect both traditional manufacturing and service jobs, and highly skilled professions. Paralegal experts, medical technicians, editors, copy writers, journalists, software engineers, administrative assistants, and people in the film and music industries, as well as drivers, call centre workers, and bank tellers are all exposed to the potential effects of AI automation. Should this process occur, without being properly managed, it would produce large-scale social dislocation and political instability.

We have already experienced a sharp rise in economic inequality throughout much of the world over the past three decades, with attendant political polarisation, extremism, and conflict.[7] Widespread unemployment due to automation would greatly intensify these patterns. How might we manage the move to a new type of economy without incurring major social disruption?

It is difficult to envisage an alternative to substantial public investment in services, and in alternative forms of employment, to protect people displaced by automation. The obvious question is where the funding to support this investment will come from. Income tax is the primary source of government revenue. If unemployment expands, then this revenue is reduced.

Corporation tax is another possible source. The problem here is that the wealthiest multinational companies frequently apply legal tax avoidance schemes to move their profits from higher to lower tax countries. Many of these are US tech companies. Taxwatch (2023) estimates that seven of these corporations avoided paying approximately £2 billion in UK corporate taxes in 2021 through such profit transfer manoeuvres. According to the Taxwatch report, these included Adobe, Alphabet (Google), Amazon, Apple, Cisco, Meta (Facebook), and Microsoft. Nair (2023) describes the mechanisms of corporate tax avoidance.[8] He also summarises a recent OECD (Organisation for Economic Co-operation and Development) proposal to constrain this practice by imposing a minimal corporate tax on all major multinationals.

When reflecting on the difficulties involved in coping with the possible economic effects of the AI revolution, it becomes apparent that individual countries are, for the most part, not in a strong position to respond to this and related problems, given the limitations of their resources and their enforcement powers. These are international issues, which require coordinated efforts within a multinational framework, to stand any chance of success. Corporate tax avoidance offers a particularly clear example. Only a common corporate tax policy adopted and enforced by leading economic powers could possibly compel wealthy corporations to pay reasonable taxes on the profits they make, in the countries in which these profits are actually generated through consumer spending on their products. Obtaining this revenue is necessary to support the redistributive programs required to mitigate the trend to severe economic inequality that the AI revolution threatens to amplify.

In this chapter, I have briefly looked at six public policy issues raised by the problems discussed in Chapter 5. These are receiving varied degrees of attention in current scientific and political discourse concerning the challenges of the AI revolution. In fact, they are all pressing. They require focussed debate and informed consideration from specialists in the field, policymakers, and the general public. How we resolve these issues will determine the way in which AI technology is integrated into our societies and how we cope with the challenges that it poses. These are not matters that we can afford to leave solely to the vicissitudes of the market, and to the tech companies that play such a dominant role in shaping that market. The public domain and its citizens need to play a major role in determining the framework within which this technology continues to develop and to be applied.

NOTES

1 See McCabe (2024) on the Google and the Microsoft cases.
2 Monti (2022) compares US and EU legislative approaches to anti-trust action against digital companies.
3 Guggenberger (2023) discusses the monopoly that tech platforms have achieved in online communication and discourse venues. Khanal et al. (2024) describe the extent to which tech companies, and AI in particular, have come to control our points of interface with government and public policymaking.
4 For a general description of federal US truth in advertising requirements, see *Truth in Advertising*, Federal Trade Commission, https://www.ftc.gov/news-events/topics/truth-advertising.
5 See, for example, Appel et al. (2023), Lucchi (2023), Picht et al. (2023), and Chesterman (2024) for discussions of different legal aspects of these issues. Sarmento (2024) addresses the ethical and legal problems that using generative AI for music composition poses.

6 Kulkarni and Nageshkumar (2020) compare the regulatory regimes on hate speech of the United States, Europe, and India. Dias (2022), and Nava and Lane (2023) suggest using human rights law, such as the International Covenant on Civil and Political Rights, to develop an international legal framework for controlling hate content. Siyuan (2024) discusses the advantages and the flaws of Singapore's POFMA as a legal mechanism for restricting online abuse.

7 Piketty (2014) provides a detailed account of the factors that have generated this rise in inequality.

8 See also the OECD press release *New OECD Data Highlight Multinational Tax Avoidance Risks and the Need for Swift Implementation of International Reform*, November 17, 2022 (https://www.oecd.org/en/about/news/press-releases/2022/11/new-oecd-data-highlight-multinational-tax-avoidance-risks-and-the-need-for-swift-implementation-of-international-reform.html).

CHAPTER 7

Conclusion

In the early years of AI researchers experimented with a diverse set of methods and frameworks in their efforts to model different aspects of human learning and reasoning. Rosenblatt's perceptrons, followed by feedforward networks, were among the first systems constructed for learning tasks. Although they were originally inspired by the structures of the human brain, artificial neural networks developed as independent formal systems whose designs are driven by computational engineering concerns. Symbolic AI yielded logic-based constraint satisfaction solvers, non-monotonic logic, Minsky frames, Schank scripts, Zadeh's fuzzy logic and set theory, as well as grammars, rewrite systems, and parsers. Statistical AI used a variety of Bayesian techniques for probabilistic reasoning and NLP (natural language processing). These included Bayesian networks and Hidden Markov Models (HMMs).

Hardware limitations and the absence of significant amounts of digital data constrained the early devices to small-scale systems with limited coverage. In most instances, they required manually produced input, as well as handcrafted extensions to cover new cases. As a result, initial excitement at the prospects for major progress alternated with disappointment and a reduction in investment. This produced an alternating sequence of AI seasons consisting in a spring of optimism, followed by a winter of scepticism. No one method or approach emerged as dominant, as each competed for influence and support.

By the end of the 1990s, hardware innovations, particularly the creation of graphics processing units (GPUs), enabled rapid training of neural networks, and it speeded up processing in general. The creation of

DOI: 10.1201/9781003624790-7

the internet provided a vast source of online digital data which opened up opportunities for wide coverage machine learning across numerous domains. These developments, combined with major changes in the architecture and training regimes of neural networks, initiated the first phase of the deep learning revolution.

Enhanced new Recurrent Neural Networks (RNNs) in the form of LSTMs (Long Short-Term Memory systems) and GRUs (Gated Recurrent Networks) applied filtering functions to select the features of input data that were retained and passed from one element of a sequence to the next. This selective processing memory facilitated the identification of long-distance relations among disparate components of the input. These networks began to yield impressive results in NLP tasks. Convolutional Neural Networks (CNNs) moved from lower-level to higher-level representations of features through a succession of pooling and convolution operations. They achieved increasing accuracy in applications like visual image recognition and classification.

DNNs operate as encoder-decoder systems in which they encode their input as vectors. They process these vectors through hidden units producing a context vector, which is transferred to the decoder to produce the output. Training consists in feeding the difference between the intended and actual outputs back through the network, and it applies a loss function to find the optimal weights for the hidden units. Much of the power of a DNN comes from its embeddings. In the case of linguistic applications, this consists of an abstract representation of the word distribution patterns extracted from the corpora on which the network is pretrained. Other distributional patterns are encoded in multimodal embeddings covering both linguistic and non-linguistic data. A DNN's embeddings provide it with the model from which it predicts the next token in its output, given the tokens that it has processed so far (in either the left or the right direction).

Adding attention to a DNN causes the context vector to be dynamically computed in a way in which previous encoding processing states are accessible, and the alignment of elements of the context vector with the decoder output is significantly refined. Transformers ushered in the second, current phase of the deep learning revolution. They consist entirely of blocks of attention heads organised in successive layers of the network. Each block is trained independently of the others, allowing for rapid parallel training. It also permits different blocks to focus on distinct features of input data and network output. Transformers have substantially improved the accuracy and the coverage of the previous generations of DNNs for most tasks. They drive the LLMs that have completely altered work in NLP and a wide variety of other applications.

There are two major types of transformers. Auto-regressive systems (such as ChatGPT) predict the next token of a sequence on the basis of the elements that precede it. The input following the current processing state is masked, and so it is not visible to the network. These are generative devices. Contextual transformers (like BERT) predict an item from the elements that provide its left and its right context. Hence, they see all tokens of the input except the contextually masked one. These models are primarily used for discrimination and classification tasks.

We have discussed some of the ways in which DNNs are creating new living and working environments. Transformers are powering chatbots that provide strikingly accurate information retrieval systems in natural language. They are able to perform a wide range of tasks involving natural language generation and editing, text organisation, and data processing. Many are multi-modal and can handle images, videos, audio files, and mathematical content.

NMT (neural machine transaltion) now provides access to high-quality machine translation across a large set of language pairs. It covers most styles and domains of text. While post-editing may still be required in some cases, NMT is starting to reach human standards of performance. Transformer-supported speech recognition and text-to-speech generation provide front and back ends for dictation applications and for commercial dialogue interface systems.

Automatic code generation applies NMT methods to mapping natural language text into computer code. It permits programmers to create, test, and correct code in a variety of languages. As DNN (Deep Neural Network) code generation improves in quality, it will replace much of the manual work in programming. This will allow software engineers to focus on high-level design and application problems, rather than the details of coding.

DNN-driven theorem proving is now producing interesting results in logic and mathematics. Some of its proofs significantly improve on those achieved by humans. It is also an effective tool for proof checking. As formal results are important for the soundness of theories in physics, and in numerous engineering applications, theorem proving is of more than theoretical interest.

Deep learning is having a profound impact on medical practice and bioinformatics. It has surpassed human performance in many diagnostic tasks, and it guides robotic surgery. It generates medical reports and recommendations from data. Transformers are able to predict proteins and protein behaviour.[1] This work has yielded important applications in pharmacology and in computational biology.

Finally, DNNs are generating visual images, videos, and musical compositions. Some of these are innovative and aesthetically interesting. In addition, DNNs are being used to identify artistic creators and to authenticate paintings. Some of the most interesting experiments in musical composition involve collaborations between generative transformers, which produce partial works of art and human interlocutors who develop and complete them. Using deep learning to create art is a new area of application. It remains to be seen to what extent it will replace human activity, or supplement it, in different modes of artistic expression. This very much depends on the reception that humans accord AI-generated and AI-assisted creations. At this point, this domain is still in an early experimental phase.

Many of the fears that futurologists have raised about AI concern the rise of superintelligent agents who would take over our environment and push humans to extinction. We looked at the history of this fear, which originates in the notion of an AI singularity. We found that this idea rests on two problematic assumptions. The first is that the rapid increase in computing hardware and processing capacity, combined with the ability to simulate human brain activity, will, in itself, create intelligent devices. In fact, the gap between complex electrical circuits, even if they approximate human neural activity, and the properties required to achieve general intelligence, remains unbridged in these claims. We argued that the problem is not the absence of internal mental states or sentience in electronic devices. These are not required for intelligent behaviour. But purposeful, volitional planning and action are emergent properties of humans (and other biological creatures), which do not simply come into being when a certain level of computational circuitry is present. While intelligence may emerge in artificial electronic circuits, it does not seem likely to do so in the foreseeable future.

The second problematic assumption concerns evaluating risk. As artificial general intelligence has never been observed before, it is not clear how we can meaningfully assess the probability of its occurrence. Singularity advocates appear to be making the mistake of inferring the likelihood of an event from its mere logical possibility. It is more rational to prioritise risks that we know to be actual and that constitute real and present dangers.

These include climate change, pandemics, wars, political extremism, poverty, and a host of other pressing problems. The singularity is not one of them.

While superintelligent artificial agents may not be a genuine concern at this point, AI has, in fact, created a host of serious problems. Some of these are not properly appreciated, in part because of the scientifically ungrounded media focus on issues like the singularity. The sharp increase in the size of transformers and the data required to train them pose significant environmental dangers. Huge amounts of energy and water are expended in these training sessions. Similarly, massive resources are needed to produce CPUs (central processing units), GPUs, and the other components of the computers that run these systems. This industry creates large quantities of toxic waste, whose disposal is problematic. The server farms that store data and support AI systems are an additional drain on power and water.

Given the massive size of large language models (LLMs), large tech companies are the only agencies that have the resources to train and operate them. This has provided them with a virtual monopoly on research in deep learning. Universities, public research institutes, and smaller start ups have become clients of these companies. They are increasingly limited to tweaking the design of these models and fine-tuning them for alternative applications. This has endowed the tech companies with control over the architecture of AI systems, and it allows them to shape the direction of research in the field. Much of the work done in these companies is of high quality and of serious scientific value. But because it is driven largely by their immediate commercial interests, important questions in basic science and engineering, which are not seen as profit generating, are being marginalised. In particular, the development of smaller and more transparent learning models that require less data to produce high performance is being neglected. Similarly, some of the questions in computational modelling of human learning and cognition, which initially inspired AI research in its earlier phases, have been largely set aside. In this respect, AI differs from physics, where large-scale public support continues to offset the cost of basic research that would not normally attract private investment.

LLMs generate high-quality natural language text and audio. They produce images and videos that are very difficult to distinguish from true representations of objects and events. They are being used to disseminate disinformation and fabricated news. This content is undermining the credibility of foundational institutions, such as free elections. It has the potential to do even greater harm on a large scale within the immediate future. Devising effective procedures to verify online digital material for factual content and reliability is now one of the major challenges in current AI research.

AI-propagated hate speech is closely related to disinformation. LLM-powered chatbots are pumping large quantities of abuse through the internet, targeting ethnic, religious, gender, and other vulnerable groups, as well as individuals. This manufactured propaganda is an inexpensive and devastatingly efficient recruiting tool for violent terrorist groups and extremists. Automatic hate speech recognition is becoming increasingly accurate. However, enforcing constraints on the propagation of this content remains a controversial issue of public policy.

Expert AI systems for assessing candidates have become pervasive in medical treatment, hiring, and the credit industry (among others). Careful study of the models that these systems employ indicates that many encode a variety of biases through their training data. In some instances, the models amplify the biases present in the data on which they are trained. Re-engineering the systems to filter out bias, while providing reliable evaluations of candidates, is far from straightforward. Solving this difficulty is imperative if this application of AI is to be both equitable and effective.

Finally, the AI revolution threatens destructive economic consequences. It is facilitating the automation of a wide spectrum of jobs across manufacturing, service industries, and highly skilled professions. Should this process produce widespread unemployment within a comparatively short period of time, it will have seriously destabilising effects. It will greatly exacerbate the already sharp rise in income inequality that we have observed over the past 30 years. Again, this is a major issue of social concern, but it has gone largely unaddressed to date.

Each of the problems created by AI summarised here (and many others) poses an important set of public policy questions. The tech companies that produce AI systems and host online services and media have achieved near monopoly status in the market for these products. Applying anti-trust measures to them involves complex legal and economic considerations. Some of these issues are now being contested in courts around the world, and they are debated in legislatures at different levels of government. The training data that the tech companies use to train their LLMs, and the products which these models generate, create copyright and ownership questions. These are fraught with subtle legal and regulatory problems that are also inspiring increasingly prominent court cases and legislative challenges.

Constraining disinformation and hate speech raises problems of principle concerning the limits of free expression. It also runs into difficulties of enforceability. Many of these stem from the multinational nature of the tech companies that host social media, the primary venues for spreading both types of content. The severe public damage that this content is causing motivates some doubt concerning the viability of a radical libertarian view on which almost all speech and publication must be entirely free of restraint.

Finally, if AI-driven automation creates large-scale economic and social dislocation, there is a strong case for public intervention to manage this process through expanded public services and alternative job creation. Declining public revenue due to corporate tax avoidance reduces the resources available for such an intervention. If handled at the level of individual governments, most countries are not in a position to respond effectively to this problem. Only coordinated international action on taxing corporate profits where they are made would seem to offer any chance of success.

The AI revolution has achieved enormous success in a comparatively short period of time in solving difficult engineering problems. It has produced major benefits across a broad range of tasks and applications. It has also created pressing environmental, social, and economic dangers. Most of the research and development responsible for current AI systems is going on in large tech companies. These have accumulated sufficient wealth and political influence to resist effective government regulation in most areas in which they operate. One of the arguments that they employ to lobby against regulation is to claim that they are socially responsible organisations best able to moderate themselves. In the 1990s, these companies were frequently presented as cool, innovative paradigms of business. Their management and their leading engineers were often regarded as clued in young entrepreneurs who pursued a more enlightened, socially responsible approach to work and commerce. The conduct of these companies over the past 20 years has exposed this image as at best naïve and without foundation.

The tech companies behave like all big businesses have throughout modern history. It would be economically self-destructive for them to do otherwise. It has been repeatedly demonstrated that markets create major damage if their actors are left to pursue profit without serious constraint from the agencies of the public interest. The current development of AI systems is a particularly clear case of the need for public regulation. It is well past time for serious discussion of how to formulate and implement the mechanisms of this regulation, to protect us from the harms of AI, while maximising its social benefit.

NOTE

1 David Baker received the 2024 Nobel Prize in Chemistry for computational protein design. He shared it with Demis Hassabis and John M. Jumper, both of Google DeepMind, who developed the AlphaFold AI system to predict a protein's structure from its amino acid sequence. In addition, John Hopfield and Geoffrey Hinton were awarded the 2024 Nobel Prize in Physics for their research on the design of neural networks and methods for deep learning.

References

Aaronson, Scott (2013), *Quantum Computing since Democritus*, Cambridge University Press, Cambridge.

Albaroudi, Elham, Taha Mansouri, and Ali Alameer (2024), "A Comprehensive Review of AI Techniques for Addressing Algorithmic Bias in Job Hiring", *AI*, Vol. 5, pp. 383–404.

ALPAC (1966), *Language and Machines: Computers in Translation and Linguistics*, Publication 1416, National Academy of Sciences and National Research Council, Washington, DC.

Appel, Gil, Juliana Neelbauer, and David A. Schweidel (2023), "Generative AI Has an Intellectual Property Problem", *Harvard Business Review*, April 7 (https://hbr.org/2023/04/generative-ai-has-an-intellectual-property-problem).

Atkinson, Cameron F. (2023), "ChatGPT and Computational-Based Research: Benefits, Drawbacks, and Machine Learning Applications", *Discover Artificial Intelligence*, Vol. 3. https://doi.org/10.1007/s44163-023-00091-3

Bahdanau, Dzmitry, KyungHyun Cho, and Yoshua Bengio (2015), "Neural Machine Translation by Jointly Learning to Align and Translate", *3rd International Conference on Learning Representations* (ICLR).

Bar-Hillel, Yehoshua (1960), "The Present Status of Automatic Translation of Languages", in Franz L. Alt (ed.), *Advances in Computers*, Elsevier, Vol. 1, pp. 91–163.

Baroni, Marco (2023), "On the Proper Role of Linguistically Oriented Deep Net Analysis in Linguistic Theorising", in Shalom Lappin and Jean-Philippe Bernardy (eds.), *Algebraic Structures in Natural Language*, Taylor and Francis, CRC Press, Boca Raton, FL and Oxford, pp. 1–16.

Bender, Emily and Alexander Koller (2020), "Climbing Towards NLU: On Meaning, Form, and Understanding in the Age of Data", *Proceedings of the 58th Annual Meeting of the Association for Computational Linguistics*, pp. 5185–5198.

Bender, Emily, Timnit Gebru, Angelina McMillan-Major, and Shmargaret Shmitchell (2021), "On the Dangers of Stochastic Parrots: Can Language Models be Too Big?", in *FAccT '21*, Association for Computing Machinery, New York, pp. 610–623.

Bernardy, Jean-Philippe, Rasmus Blanck, Stergios Chatzikyriakidis, Shalom Lappin, and Aleksandre Maskharashvili (2022), "Bayesian Inference Semantics for Natural Language", in Jean-Philippe Bernardy, Rasmus Blanck, Stergios

Chatzikyriakidis, Shalom Lappin, and Aleksandre Maskharashvili (eds.), *Probabilistic Approaches to Linguistic Theory*, CSLI Publications, Stanford, CA, pp. 161–228.

Bernardy, Jean-Phillipe and Shalom Lappin (2017), "Using Deep Neural Networks to Learn Syntactic Agreement", *Linguistic Issues in Language Technology*, Vol. 15. https://aclanthology.org/2017.lilt-15.3/

Bernardy, Jean-Philippe and Shalom Lappin (2023), "Unitary Recurrent Networks", in Shalom Lappin and Jean-Philippe Bernardy (eds.), *Algebraic Structures in Natural Language*, Taylor and Francis, CRC Press, Boca Raton, FL and Oxford, pp. 243–277.

Bissell, Christopher (2009), "A History of Automatic Control", in Shimon Y. Nof (ed.), *Springer Handbook of Automation*, Springer, Berlin and Heidelberg, pp. 53–69.

Bizzoni, Yuri and Shalom Lappin (2018), "Predicting Human Metaphor Paraphrase Judgments with Deep Neural Networks", *Proceedings of the ACL Workshop on Figurative Language Processing*, New Orleans, LA, pp. 45–55.

Bofill, Miquel, Miquel Palahí, Josep Suy, and Mateu Villaret (2012), "Solving Constraint Satisfaction Problems with SAT Modulo Theories", *Constraints*, Vol. 17, pp. 273–303.

Bostrom, Nick (2014), *Superintelligence: Paths, Dangers, Strategies*, Oxford University Press, Oxford and New York.

Bowman, Sam, Gabor Angeli, Christopher Potts, and Christopher D. Manning (2015), "A Large Annotated Corpus for Learning Natural Language Inference", *Proceedings of the 2015 Conference on Empirical Methods in Natural Language Processing (EMNL)*, Lisbon, Portugal, pp. 632–642.

Broniatowski, David A., Joseph R. Simons, Jiayan Gu, Amelia M. Jamison, and Lorien C. Abroms (2023), "The Efficacy of Facebook's Vaccine Misinformation Policies and Architecture during the COVID-19 Pandemic", *Science Advances*, Vol. 9, pp. 1–17.

Brown, Peter F., John Cocke, Stephen A. Della Pietra, Vincent J. Della Pietra, Fredrick Jelinek, John D. Lafferty, Robert L. Mercer, and Paul S. Roossin (1990), "A Statistical Approach to Machine Translation", *Computational Linguistics*, Vol. 16, No. 2, pp. 79–85.

Brown, Tom B., Benjamin Mann, Nick Ryder, Melanie Subbiah, Jared Kaplan, Prafulla Dhariwa, Arvind Neelakantan, Pranav Shyam, Girish Sastry, Amanda Askell, Sandhini Agarwal, Ariel Herbert-Voss, Gretchen Krueger, Tom Henighan, Rewon Child, Aditya Ramesh, Daniel M. Ziegler, Jeffrey Wu, Clemens Winter, Christopher Hesse, Mark Chen, Eric Sigler, Mateusz Litwin, Scott Gray, Benjamin Chess, Jack Clark, Christopher Berner, Sam McCandlish, Alec Radford, Ilya Sutskever, and Dario Amodei (2020), "Language Models are Few-Shot Learners", *arXiv* 2005.14165.

Brynjolfsson, Erik and Andrew McAfee (2014), *The Second Machine Age: Work, Progress, and Prosperity in a Time of Brilliant Technologies*, W.W. Norton and Co.

Chalmers, David (1996), *The Conscious Mind*, Oxford University Press, Oxford and New York.

Chandra, Abel, Laura Tünnermann, Tommy Löfstedt, and Regina Gratz (2023), "Transformer- Based Deep Learning for Predicting Protein Properties in the Life Sciences", *eLife*, Vol. 12. https://doi.org/10.7554/eLife.82819c

Chen, Wenjie, Xiaoting Huang, Xueting Liu, Huisi Wu, and Fu Qi (2023), "Authenticity Identification of Qi Baishi's Shrimp Painting with Dynamic Token Enhanced Visual Transformer", *Advances in Computer Graphics: 39th Computer Graphics International Conference*, Springer, Berlin and Heidelberg, pp. 554–565.

Chesterman, Simon (2024), "Good Models Borrow, Great Models Steal: Intellectual Property Rights and Generative AI", *Policy and Society*. https://doi.org/10.1093/polsoc/puae006

Cho, Kyunghyun, Bart van Merriënboer, Caglar Gulcehre, Dzmitry Bahdanau, Fethi Bougares, Holger Schwenk, and Yoshua Bengio (2014), "Learning Phrase Representations Using RNN Encoder–Decoder for Statistical Machine Translation", *Proceedings of the 2014 Conference on Empirical Methods in Natural Language Processing (EMNLP)*, ACL, Doha, Qatar, pp. 1724–1734.

Chomsky, Noam (1957), *Syntactic Structures*, Mouton, The Hague.

Chomsky, Noam, Ian Roberts, and Jeffrey Watumull (2023), "The False Promise of ChatGPT", The New York Times, March 8, 2023.

Clark, Alexander and Shalom Lappin (2011), *Linguistic Nativism and Poverty of Stimulus*, Wiley-Blackwell, Malden, MA and Oxford.

DeepSeek-AI (2024a), "DeepSeek-V2: A Strong, Economical, and Efficient Mixture-of-Experts Language Model", *arXiv* 2405.04434.

DeepSeek-AI (2024b), "DeepSeek-V3 Technical Report", *arXiv* 2412.19437v1.

DeepSeek-AI (2025), "DeepSeek-R1: Incentivizing Reasoning Capability in LLMs via Reinforcement Learning", *arXiv* 2501.12948.

Devlin, Jacob, Ming-Wei Chang, Kenton Lee, and Kristina Toutanova (2019), "BERT: Pre-training of Deep Bidirectional Transformers for Language Understanding", *Proceedings of NAACL-HLT 2019*, ACL, Minneapolis, MN, pp. 4171–4186.

Dias, Talita (2022), "Tackling Online Hate Speech through Content Moderation: The Legal Framework under the International Covenant on Civil and Political Rights", *Blavatnik School of Government (BSG) Working Papers Series*, Oxford Institute for Ethics, Law and Armed Conflict.

Dong, Hao-Wen, Ke Chen, Shlomo Dubnov, Julian McAuley, and Taylor Berg-Kirkpatrick (2023), "Multitrack Music Transformer", *Proceedings of the IEEE International Conference on Acoustics, Speech and Signal Processing (ICASSP)*, IEEE.

Dubhashi, Devdatt and Shalom Lappin (2017), "AI Dangers: Imagined and Real", *Communications of the ACM*, Vol. 60, No. 2, pp. 43–45.

Eberhart, R. C. and R. W. Dobbins (1990, September), "Early Neural Network Development History: The Age of Camelot", *IEEE Xplore: Engineering in Medicine and Biology*, Vol. 9, No. 3, pp. 15–18.

Elman, Jeffrey (1990), "Finding Structure in Time", *Cognitive Science*, Vol. 14, pp. 179–211.

Elman, Jeffrey (1991), "Distributed Representations, Simple Recurrent Networks, and Grammatical Structure", *Machine Learning*, Vol. 7, pp. 195–225.

Elman, Jeffrey (1998), "Generalization, Simple Recurrent Networks, and the Emergence of Structure", in M. Gernsbacher and S. Derry (eds.), *Proceedings of the 20th Annual Conference of the Cognitive Science Society*, Lawrence Erlbaum Associates, Mahway, NJ.

Espejel, Jessica López, Mahaman Sanoussi Yahaya Alassan, El Mehdi Chouham, Walid Mahhane, and El Hassane Ettifouri (2023), "A Comprehensive Review of State-of-The-Art Methods for Java Code Generation from Natural Language Text", *Natural Language Processing Journal*, Vol. 3, No. 2, pp. 1–16.

Fathullah, Yassir, Chunyang Wu, Egor Lakomkin, Junteng Jia, Yuan Shangguan, Ke Li, Jinxi Guo, Wenhan Xiong, Jay Mahadeokar, Ozlem Kalinli, Christian Fuegen, and Mike Seltzer (2024), "Prompting Large Language Models with Speech Recognition Abilities", *IEEE International Conference on Acoustics, Speech, and Signal Processing (ICASSP)*, IEEE.

Ferrara, Emilio (2024), "Fairness and Bias in Artificial Intelligence: A Brief Survey of Sources, Impacts, and Mitigation Strategies", *Sci*, Vol. 6, No. 1:3. https://doi.org/10.3390/sci6010003

Fitting, Melvin (1996), *First-Order Logic and Automated Theorem Proving*, Springer, New York, NY.

Fosler-Lussier, Eric (1998), *Markov Models and Hidden Markov Models: A Brief Tutorial*, International Computer Science Institute, Berkeley, CA.

Gambín, Ángel Fernández, Anis Yazidi, Athanasios Vasilakos, Hårek Haugerud, and Youcef Djenouri (2024), "Deepfakes: Current and Future Trends", *Artificial Intelligence Review*, Vol. 57. https://doi.org/10.1007/s10462-023-10679-x

Garcia, Ana Cristina Bicharra, Marcio Gomes Pinto Garcia, and Roberto Rigobon (2024), "Algorithmic Discrimination in the Credit Domain: What Do We Know about It?", *AI & Society*, Vol. 39, pp. 2059–2098.

Garcia, Xavier, Yamini Bansal, Colin Cherry, George Foster, Maxim Krikun, Melvin Johnson, and Orhan Firat (2023), "The Unreasonable Effectiveness of Few-shot Learning for Machine Translation", *Proceedings of the 40th International Conference on Machine Learning*, Vol. 202. https://proceedings.mlr.press/v202/garcia23a.html

Gilardi, Fabrizio, Meysam Alizadeh, and Maël Kubli (2023), "ChatGPT Outperforms Crowd Workers for Text-Annotation Tasks", *Proceedings of the National Academy of Science*, Vol. 120, No. 30. https://doi.org/10.1073/pnas.2305016120

Goldberg, Yoav (2019), "Assessing BERT's Syntactic Abilities", *arXiv*:abs/1901.05287.

Good, Irving John (1953), "The Population Frequencies of Species and the Estimation of Population Parameters", Biometrika, Vol. 40, No. 3/4, pp. 237–264.

Good, Irving John (1966), "Speculations Concerning the First Ultraintelligent Machine", in Franz L. Alt and Morris Rubinoff (eds.), Advances in Computers, Elsevier, Vol. 6, pp. 31–88.

Green, Andrew (2024), *Artificial Intelligence and the Changing Demand for Skills in the Labour Market*, OECD Artificial Intelligence Papers, No. 14, OECD Publishing, Paris.

Grishman, Ralph (2010), "Information Extraction", in Alexander Clark, Chis Fox, and Shalom Lappin (eds.), *The Handbook of Computational Linguistics and Natural Language Processing*, Wiley-Blackwell, Oxford, Hoboken, NJ, pp. 517–530.

Guggenberger, Nikolas (2023), "Moderating Monopolies", *Berkeley Technology Law Journal*, Vol. 38, pp. 119–172.

Gupta, Tushar (2017, January 5), "Deep Learning: Feedforward Neural Network", *Toward Data Science*.

Gulordava, Kristina, Piotr Bojanowski, Edouard Grave, Tal Linzen, and Marco Baroni (2018), "Colorless Green Recurrent Networks Dream Hierarchically", *Proceedings of the 2018 Conference of the North American Chapter of the Association for Computational Linguistics: Human Language Technologies*, Vol. 1, pp. 1195–1205.

Häggström, Olle (2016), *Here Be Dragons*, Oxford University Press, Oxford and New York.

Halper, Evan and Caroline O'Donovan (2024), "AI is Exhausting the Power Grid: Tech Firms are Seeking a Miracle Solution", *The Washington Post*, June 21, 2024 (https://www.washingtonpost.com/business/2024/06/21/artificial-intelligence-nuclear-fusion-climate/).

Halpern, Joseph (2003), *Reasoning about Uncertainty*, MIT Press, Cambridge, MA.

Han, Jesse Michael, Igor Babuschkin, Harrison Edwards, Arvind Neelakantan, Tao Xu, Stanislas Polu, Alex Ray, Pranav Shyam, Aditya Ramesh, Alec Radford, and Ilya Sutskever (2021), "Unsupervised Neural Machine Translation with Generative Language Models Only", *arXiv* 2110.05448.

Harnad, Stevan (1990), "The Symbol Grounding Problem", *Physica D*, Vol. 42, Nos. 1–3, pp. 335–346.

Hewitt, John and Christopher D. Manning (2019), "A Structural Probe for Finding Syntax in Word Representations", *Proceedings of the 2019 Conference of the North American Chapter of the Association for Computational Linguistics: Human Language Technologies*, Vol. 1 (Long and Short Papers), pp. 4129–4138.

Hochreiter, Sepp and Jürgen Schmidhuber (1997), "Long Short-Term Memory", *Neural Computation*, Vol. 9, No. 8, pp. 1735–1780.

Honkela, Antti (2001), *Nonlinear Switching State-Space Models*, MSc Thesis, Helsinki University of Technology.

Horev, Rani (2018), "BERT- State of the Art Language Model for NLP", *Lyrn.AI*, November 7, 2018.

Hwang, JaeYoung and SangHoon Oh (2023), "A Brief Survey of Watermarks in Generative AI", *14th International Conference on Information and Communication Technology*, IEEE, pp. 1157–1160.

Jelinek, Frederick (1995), "Training and Search Methods for Speech Recognition", *Proceedings of the National Academy of Science USA*, Vol. 92, pp. 9964–9969.

Jelinek, Frederick (1998), *Statistical Methods for Speech Recognition*, MIT Press, Cambridge, MA.

Jelinek, Frederick, Lalit R. Bahl, and Robert Mercer (1975), "Design of a Linguistic Statistical Decoder for the Recognition of Continuous Speech", *IEEE Transactions on Information Theory*, Vol. IT-21, No. 3, pp. 250–256.

Jiang, Albert Q., Alexandre Sablayrolles, Arthur Mensch, Chris Bamford, Devendra Singh Chaplot, Diego de las Casas, Florian Bressand, Gianna Lengyel, Guillaume Lample, Lucile Saulnier, Lélio Renard Lavaud, Marie-Anne Lachaux, Pierre Stock, Teven Le Scao, Thibaut Lavril, Thomas Wang, Timothée Lacroix, William El Sayed (2023), "Mistral 7B", *arXiv* 2310.06825.

Joshi, Aravind, K. Vijay Shanker, and David Weir (1990), *The Convergence of Mildly Context- Sensitive Grammar Formalisms*, Technical Report, Department of Computer and Information Science, University of Pennsylvania.

Jung, Carsten and Bhargav Srinivasa Desikan (2023), *Transformed by AI: How Generative Artificial Intelligence Could Transform Work in the UK- and How to Manage It*, Institute for Public Policy Research (IPPR), London.

Jurafsky, Daniel and James Martin (2023), *Speech and Language Processing*, third edition draft, Stanford University, Stanford, CA.

Kamalloo, Ehsan, Nouha Dziri, Charles L. A. Clarke, and Davood Rafiei (2023), "Evaluating Open-Domain Question Answering in the Era of Large Language Models", *Proceedings of the 61st Annual Meeting of the Association for Computational Linguistics, Volume 1: Long*, Association for Computational Linguistics, Toronto, Canada, pp. 5591–5606.

Khan, Lina M. (2017), "Amazon's Antitrust Paradox", *The Yale Law Journal*, Vo. 126, pp. 710–805.

Khanal, Shaleen, Hongzhou Zhang, and Araz Taeihagh (2024), "Why and How Is the Power of Big Tech Increasing in the Policy Process? The Case of Generative AI", *Policy and Society*. https://doi.org/10.1093/polsoc/puae012

Kim, Sehoon, Amir Gholam, Albert Shaw, Nicholas Lee, Karttikeya Mangalam, Jitendra Malik, Michael W. Mahoney, and Kurt Keutzer (2022), "Squeezeformer: An Efficient Transformer for Automatic Speech Recognition", *Proceedings of 36th Conference on Neural Information Processing Systems* NeurIPS.

Kimm, Haklin, Incheon Paik, and Hanke Kimm (2021), "Performance Comparision of TPU, *GPU, CPU on Google Colaboratory over Distributed Deep Learning*", *2021 IEEE 14th International Symposium on Embedded Multicore/Many-core Systems-on-Chip* MCSoC. https://ieeexplore.ieee.org/document/9691951

Kirtley, Jane (2018), "Getting to the Truth: Fake News, Libel Laws, and 'Enemies of the American People'", *Human Rights*, Vol. 43, No. 4, American Bar Association (https://www.americanbar.org/groups/crsj/publications/human_rights_magazine_home/the-ongoing-challenge-to-define-free-speech/getting-to-the-truth/).

Kneser, Reinhard and Hermann Ney (1995), "Improved Backing-Off for M-Gram Language Modeling", *IEEE International Conference on Acoustics, Speech, and Signal Processing*, Vol. 1, pp. 181–184.

Knight, Will (2023), "OpenAI's CEO Says the Age of Giant AI Models Is Already Over", *Wired*, April 17.

Kulkarni, Rahul Shantanu and Spandana Nageshkumar (2020), "Regulating Online Hate Speech: A Comparative Study of the United States of America, European Union and India's Approaches", *International Journal of Legal Science and Innovation*, Vol. 2, No. 2. pp. 55–69.

Kumarage, Tharindu, Amrita Bhattacharjee, and Joshua Garland (2024), "Harnessing Artificial Intelligence to Combat Online Hate: Exploring the Challenges and Opportunities of Large Language Models in Hate Speech Detection", *arXiv* 2403.08035.

Kurzweil, Ray (1999), *The Age of Spiritual Machines*, Textere, New York and London.

Kurzweil, Ray (2006), *The Singularity Is Near: When Humans Transcend Biology*, Duckworth, London.

Lample, Guillaume, Marie-Anne Lachaux, Thibaut Lavril, Xavier Martinet, Amaury Hayat, Gabriel Ebner, Aurélien Rodriguez, and Timothée Lacroix (2022), "HyperTree Proof Search for Neural Theorem Proving", *36th Conference on Neural Information Processing Systems*. NeurIPS.

Lappin, Shalom (2018), "Towards a Computationally Viable Framework for Semantic Representation", *Proceedings of the Symposium on Logic and Algorithms in Computational Linguistics 2018*, Stockholm University, DiVA Portal for digital publications, pp. 47–63.

Lappin, Shalom (2021), *Deep Learning and Linguistic Representation*, Taylor and Francis, CRC, Oxford and Boca Raton.

Lappin, Shalom (2024), "Assessing the Strengths and Weaknesses of Large Language Models", *Journal of Logic, Language and Information*, special issue Natural Logic Meets Machine Learning, Vol. 33, pp. 9–20.

Lappin, Shalom (2025), *Neuro-Symbolic Models in AI*, talk presented to the seminar of the Centre for Linguistic Theory and Studies in Probability, University of Gothenburg, February 27, 2025 (slides available at https://gu-clasp.github.io/events/seminars/2025-02-27-seminar-by-shalom-lappin/Shalom%20Lappin%2027.2.2025.pdf).

Lappin, Shalom and Stuart Shieber (2007), "Machine Learning Theory and Practice as a Source of Insight into Universal Grammar", *Journal of Linguistics*, Vol. 43, pp. 393–427.

Lasri, Karim (2023), *Linguistic Generalization in Transformer-Based Neural Language Models*, unpublished PhD thesis, l'École Normale Supérieure, University of Paris.

Lau, Jey Han, Alexander Clark, and Shalom Lappin (2017), "Grammaticality, Acceptability, and Probability: A Probabilistic View of Linguistic Knowledge", *Cognitive Science*, Vol. 41, No. 5, pp. 1202–1241.

Lau, Jey Han, Carlos Armendariz, Shalom Lappin, Matthew Purver, and Chang Shu (2020), "How Furiously Can Colorless Green Ideas Sleep? Sentence Acceptability in Context", *Transactions of the Association for Computational Linguistics*, Vol. 8, pp. 296–310.

Le, Matthew, Apoorv Vyas, Bowen Shi, Brian Karrer, Leda Sari, Rashel Moritz, Mary Williamson, Vimal Manohar, Yossi Adi, Jay Mahadeokar, and Wei-Ning Hsu (2023), "Voicebox: Text-Guided Multilingual Universal Speech Generation at Scale", *37th Conference on Neural Information Processing Systems (NeurIPS 2023)*. IEEE.

LeCun, Yann, Koray Kavukcuoglu, and Clement Farabet (2010), "Convolutional Networks and Applications in Vision", *Proceedings of 2010 IEEE International Symposium on Circuits and Systems*, IEEE, pp. 253–256.

Lev-Ram, Michal (2024), "The Chip Industry's Dirty Little Secret: It's Very Dirty", *Fortune*, January 29.

Lewis, Patrick, Ethan Perez, Aleksandra Piktus, Fabio Petroni, Vladimir Karpukhin, Naman Goyal, Heinrich Küttler, Mike Lewis, Wen-tau Yih, Tim Rocktäschel, Sebastian Riedel, and Douwe Kiela (2020), "Retrieval- Augmented Generation for Knowledge- Intensive NLP Tasks", *34th Conference on Neural Information Processing Systems (NeurIPS 2020)*, NeurIPS. pp. 9459–9474.

Li, Chuan (2020), "OpenAI's GPT-3 Language Model: A Technical Overview", *Lambda*, June 3.

Lighthill, James (1973), *Artificial Intelligence: A General Survey*, Report submitted to the Science Research Council, Cambridge University, Cambridge.

Linzen, Tal, Emmanuel Dupoux, and Yoav Goldberg (2016), "Assessing the Ability of LSTMs to Learn Syntax-Sensitive Dependencies", *Transactions of the Association for Computational Linguistics*, Vol. 4, pp. 521–535.

Loth, Alexander, Martin Kappes, and Marc-Oliver Pahl (2024), "Blessing or Curse? A Survey on the Impact of Generative AI on Fake News", *arXiv* 2404.03021.

Lu, Jiasen, Dhruv Batra, Devi Parikh, and Stefan Lee (2019), "ViLBERT: Pretraining Task-Agnostic Visiolinguistic Representations for Vision-and-Language Tasks", *Proceedings of the 33rd International Conference on Neural Information Processing Systems*, NeuroIPS, pp. 13–23.

Lubbad, Mohammed (2023), "GPT-4 Parameters: The Future of Natural Language Processing", *Medium*, March 24.

Lucchi, Nicola (2023), "ChatGPT: A Case Study on Copyright Challenges for Generative Artificial Intelligence Systems", *European Journal of Risk Regulation*. https://www.cambridge.org/core/journals/european-journal-of-risk-regulation/article/chatgpt-a-case-study-on-copyright-challenges-for-generative-artificial-intelligence-systems/CEDCE34DED599CC4EB20 1289BB161965

Mackworth, Alan (1992), "The Logic of Constraint Satisfaction", *Artificial Intelligence*, Vol. 58, Nos. 1–3, pp. 3–20.

Mahowald, Kyle, Anna A. Ivanova, Idan A. Blank, Nancy Kanwisher, Joshua L. Tenenbaum, and Evelina Fedorenko (2024), "Dissociating Language and Thought in Large Language Models", *Trends in Cognitive Science*, pp. 517–540.

Manning, Christopher and Hinrich Schütze (1999), *Foundations of Statistical Natural Language Processing*, MIT Press, Cambridge, MA.

Marcus, Gary (2022), "Deep Learning Alone Isn't Getting Us to Human-Like AI", *Noema*.

McCabe, David (2024), "'Google Is a Monopolist,' Judge Rules in Landmark Antitrust Case", *New York Times*, August 5, 2024.

McClelland, James L. (2016), "Capturing Gradience, Continuous Change, and Quasi- Regularity in Sound, Word, Phrase, and Meaning", in Brian MacWhinney and William O'Grady (eds.), *The Handbook of Language Emergence*, John Wiley and Sons, Hoboken NJ, pp. 54–80.

McCulloch, Warren and Walter Pitts (1943), "A Logical Calculus of the Ideas Immanent in Nervous Activity", *Bulletin of Mathematical Biology*, Vol. 52, No. 1/2, pp. 99–115.

Mendelsohn, Elliot (2015), *Introduction to Mathematical Logic*, sixth edition, Routledge, London.

Mikolov, Thomas, Kai Chen, Greg Corrado, and Jeffrey Dean (2013), "Efficient Estimation of Word Representations in Vector Space", *arXiv* 1301.3781 [cs.CL].

Minde, Tor Björn (2023), "Generative AI Does Not Run on Thin Air!", *RISE Blog*, October 8.

Minsky, Marvin (1974), *A Framework for Representing Knowledge*, MIT-AI Laboratory Memo 306, June, 1974, MIT, Cambridge, MA.

Minsky, Marvin (1991), "Logical versus Analogical or Symbolic versus Connectionist or Neat versus Scruffy", *AI Magazine*, Vol. 12, No. 2, pp. 34–51.

Minsky, Marvin and Seymour Papert (1969), *Perceptrons*, MIT Press, Cambridge, MA.

Monti, Giorgio (2022), "Taming Digital Monopolies: A Comparative Account of the Evolution of Antitrust and Regulation in the European Union and the United States", *The Antitrust Bulletin*, Vol. 67, No. 1, pp. 40–68.

Moore, Gordon (1965), "Cramming More Components onto Integrated Circuits", *Electronics*, Vol. 38, No. 8, pp. 33–35.

Nair, Vedanth (2023), "How Is the World Tackling Tax Avoidance by Multinational Companies?", *Institute for Fiscal Studies*, March 17 (https://ifs.org.uk/articles/how-world-tackling-tax-avoidance-multinational-companies).

Narayanan, Deepak, Mohammad Shoeybi, Jared Casper, Patrick LeGresley, Mostofa Patwary, Vijay Korthikanti, Dmitri Vainbrand, and Bryan Catanzaro (2021), "Scaling Language Model Training to a Trillion Parameters Using Megatron", *NVIDIA Developer: Technical Blog*, April 12.

Nava, Eva and Lottie Lane (2023), "Countering Online Hate Speech: How Does Human Rights Due Diligence Impact Terms of Service?", *Computer Law & Security Review*, Vol. 51, pp. 1–18.

Nazer, Lama H., Razan Zatarah, Shai Waldrip, Janny Xue Chen Ke, Mira Moukheiber, Ashish K. Khanna, Rachel S. Hicklen, Lama Moukheiber, Dana Moukheiber, Haobo Ma, and Piyush Mathur (2023), "Bias in Artificial Intelligence Algorithms and Recommendations for Mitigation", *PLOS Digital Health*, June 22.

Nivre, Joachim (2006), *Dependency Parsing*, Springer, Berlin.

Norvig, Peter and Stuart Russell (2020), *Artificial Intelligence: A Modern Approach*, fourth edition, Pearson, London.

OECD (2023), *OECD Employment Outlook 2023: Artificial Intelligence and the Labour Market*, OECD Publishing, Paris.

OpenAI (2023), "GPT-4 Technical Report", *arXiv*:2303.08774.

Papadimitriou, C. (1995), *Computational Complexity*, Addison-Wesley Publishing Co., Reading, MA.

Parker, Sara and Derek Ruths (2023), "Is Hate Speech Detection the Solution the World Wants?", Proceedings of the National Academy of Science, Vol. 120, No. 10, pp. 1–5.

Pascanu, Razvan, Tomas Mikolov, and Yoshua Bengio (2013), "On the Difficulty of Training Recurrent Neural Networks", *Proceedings of the 30th International Conference on Machine Learning*.

Pearl, Judea and Stuart Russell (2003), "Bayesian Networks", in M. A. Arbib (ed.), *Handbook of Brain Theory and Neural Networks*, MIT Press, Cambridge, MA pp. 157–160.

Pendzel, Sagi, Tomer Wullach, Amir Adler, and Einat Minkov (2023), "Generative AI for Hate Speech Detection: Evaluation and Findings", arXiv: 2311.09993.

Pennington, Jeffrey, Richard Socher, and Christopher D. Manning (2014), "GloVe: Global Vectors for Word Representation", *Proceedings of the 2014 Conference on Empirical Methods in Natural Language Processing (EMNLP)*, ACL, Dohar, Qatar, pp. 1532–1543.

Pereira, Fernando (2000), "Formal Grammar and Information Theory: Together Again?", in *Philosophical Transactions of the Royal Society*, Royal Society, London, pp. 1239–1253.

Pereira, Fernando and David Warren (1980), "Definite Clause Grammars for Language Analysis- A Survey of the Formalism and a Comparison with Augmented Transition Networks", *Artificial Intelligence*, Vol. 13, No. 3, pp. 231–278.

Piantadosi, Steven (2023), "Modern Language Models Refute Chomsky's Approach to Language", Lingbuzz Preprint, *Lingbuzz 7180*.

Picht, Peter Georg and Florent Thouvenin (2023), "AI and IP: Theory to Policy and Back Again – Policy and Research Recommendations at the Intersection of Artificial Intelligence and Intellectual Property", *IIC - International Review of Intellectual Property and Competition Law*, Vol. 54, pp. 916–940.

Piketty, Thomas (2014), *Capital in the Twenty-first Century*, Harvard University Press, Cambridge, MA.

Poibeau, Thierry (2017), "The 1966 ALPAC Report and Its Consequences", in *Machine Translation*, MIT Press, Cambridge, MA, pp. 75–89.

Polu, Stanislas and Ilya Sutskever (2020), "Generative Language Modeling for Automated Theorem Proving", *arXiv*: 2009.03393.

Rajan, Mira T. Sundara (2024), "Is Generative AI Fair Use of Copyright Works? NYT v. OpenAI", *Kluwer Copyright Blog*, February 29 (https://copyrightblog.kluweriplaw.com/2024/02/29/is-generative-ai-fair-use-of-copyright-works-nyt-v-openai/).

Reiter, Raymond (1987), "Nonmonotonic Reasoning", *Annual Review of Computer Science*, Vol. 2, pp. 147–186.

Rosenblatt, Frank (1957), *The Perceptron A Perceiving and Recognising Automaton* (Project Para), Cornell Aeronautical Laboratory, Report 85-460-1.

Rosenblatt, Frank (1959), "Two Theorems of Statistical Separability in the Perceptron", in *Mechanization of Thought Processes: Proceedings of a Symposium Held at the National Physical Laboratory*, November, 1958, HM Stationery Office, London, Vol. 1, pp. 421–456.

Rumelhart, David E., Geoffrey E. Hinton, and Ronald J. Williams (1986a), "Learning Representations by Back-Propagating Errors", *Nature*, Vol. 323, pp. 533–536.

Rumelhart, David E., James L. McClelland, and the PDP Research Group (eds.) (1986b), *Parallel Distributed Processing: Explorations in the Microstructure of Cognition, Vol. 1: Foundations*, MIT Press, Cambridge, MA.

Sanderson, Mark and Bruce Croft (2012), "The History of Information Retrieval Research", *Proceedings of the IEEE*, IEEE, pp. 1444–1451.

Sarmento, Pedro Pereira (2024), *Guitar Tablature Generation with Deep Learning*, unpublished PhD thesis, School of Electronic Engineering and Computer Science, Queen Mary University of London.

Saul, Josh and Dina Bass (2023), "Artificial Intelligence Is Booming- So Is Its Carbon Footprint", *Bloomberg*, March 9.

Schaerf, Ludovica, Eric Postma, and Carina Popovici (2023), "Art Authentication with Vision Transformers", *Neural Computing and Applications*, pp. 11849–11858.

Schank, Roger and Robert Abelson (1977), *Scripts, Plans, Goals and Understanding: An Inquiry into Human Knowledge Structures*, Lawrence Erlbaum, Mahwah, NJ.

Searle, John (1980), "Minds, Brains, and Programs", *Behavioral and Brain Sciences*, Vol. 3, No. 3, pp. 417–424.

Searle, John (2014), "What Your Computer Can't Know", *New York Review of Books*, October 9.

Shamshad, Fahad, Salman Khan, Syed Waqas Zamir, Muhammad Haris Khan, Munawar Hayat, Fahad Shahbaz Khan, and Huazhu Fu (2023), "Transformers in Medical Imaging: A Survey", *Medical Image Analysis*, Vol. 88. https://doi.org/10.1016/j.media.2023.102802

Shattock, Ethan (2021), "Self-Regulation 2:0? A Critical Reflection of the European Fight Against Disinformation", *Harvard Kennedy School Misinformation Review*, Vol. 2, No. 3. https://doi.org/10.37016/mr-2020-73

Shieber, Stuart (1985), "Evidence against the Context-Freeness of Natural Language", *Linguistics and Philosophy*, Vol. 8, No. 3, pp. 333–343.

Shieber, Stuart (ed.) (2004), *The Turing Test*, MIT Press, Cambridge, MA.

Shih, Yi-Jen, Shih-Lun Wu, Frank Zalkow, Meinard Müller, and Yi-Hsuan Yang (2022), "Theme Transformer: Symbolic Music Generation with Theme-Conditioned Transformer", *IEEE Transactions on Multimedia*, Vol. 25, pp. 3495–3508.

Shoaib, Mohamed R., Zefan Wang, Milad Taleby Ahvanooey, and Jun Zhao (2023), "Deepfakes, Misinformation, and Disinformation in the Era of Frontier AI, Generative AI, and Large AI Models", *2023 International Conference on Computer and Applications (ICCA)*, IEEE.

Silverman, Craig, Craig Timberg, Jeff Kao, and Jeremy B. Merrill (2022), "Facebook Hosted Surge of Misinformation and Insurrection Threats in Months Leading Up to Jan. 6 Attack, Records Show", *ProPublica*, January 4, 2022 (https://www.propublica.org/article/facebook-hosted-surge-of-misinformation-and-insurrection-threats-in-months-leading-up-to-jan-6-attack-records-show).

Siyuan, Chen (2024), "Regulating Online Hate Speech: The Singapore Experiment", *International Review of Law, Computers & Technology*, Vol. 38, No. 2, pp. 119–139.

Smolensky, Paul (1987), "Connectionist AI, Symbolic AI, and the Brain", *Artificial Intelligence Review*, Vol. 1, No. 2, pp. 95–109.

Solaiman, Irene, Miles Brundage, Jack Clark, Amanda Askell, Ariel Herbert-Voss, Jeff Wu, Alec Radford, Gretchen Krueger, Jong Wook Kim, Sarah Kreps, Miles McCain, Alex Newhouse, Jason Blazakis, Kris McGuffie, and Jasmine Wang (2019), "Release Strategies and the Social Impacts of Language Models", *arXiv:* 1908.09203.

Soliman, Ahmed, Samir Shaheen, and Mayada Hadhoud (2024), "Leveraging Pre-Trained Language Models for Code Generation", *Complex & Intelligent Systems*, Vol. 10, pp. 3955–3980.

Soltani, Reza, Marzia Zaman, Rohit Joshi, and Srinivas Sampalli (2022), "Distributed Ledger Technologies and Their Applications: A Review", *Applied Sciences*, Vol. 12. https://doi.org/10.3390/app12157898

Stahlberg, Felix (2020), "Neural Machine Translation: A Review", *Journal of Artificial Intelligence Research*, Vol. 69, pp. 343–418.

Talman, Aarne, Marianna Apidianaki, Stergios Chatzikyriakidis, and Jorg Tiedemann (2021), "NLI Data Sanity Check: Assessing the Effect of Data Corruption on Model Performance", *Proceedings of the 23rd Nordic Conference on Computational Linguistics* NoDaLiDa, pp. 276–287.

Talman, Aarne and Stergios Chatzikyriakidis (2019), "Testing the Generalization Power of Neural Network Models across NLI Benchmarks", *Proceedings of the 2019 ACL Workshop BlackboxNLP: Analyzing and Interpreting Neural Networks for NLP*, ACL, Florence, Italy, pp. 85–94.

Tamura, Naoyuki, Tomoya Tanjo, and Mutsunori Banbara (2010), "Solving Constraint Satisfaction Problems with SAT Technology", in *FLOPS 10, Functional and Logic Programming*, Springer, Berlin and Heidelberg, pp. 19–23.

Tan, Corinne (2022), "The Curious Case of Regulating False News on Google", *Computer Law and Security Review*, Vol. 6, pp. 1–14.

Taxwatch (2023), "Seven Large Tech Groups Estimated to Have Dodged £2bn in UK Tax in 2021", October 16 (https://www.taxwatchuk.org/seven-large-tech-groups-estimated-to-have-dodged-2bn-in-uk-tax-in-2021/).

Touvron, Hugo, Thibaut Lavril, Gautier Izacard, Xavier Martinet, Marie-Anne Lachaux, Timothee Lacroix, Baptiste Rozière, Naman Goyal, Eric Hambro, Faisal Azhar, Aurelien Rodriguez, Armand Joulin, Edouard Grave, and Guillaume Lample (2023), "LLaMA: Open and Efficient Foundation Language Models", *arXiv:* 2302.13971v1.

Turing, Alan M. (1936), "On Computable Numbers, with an Application to the Entscheidungsproblem", *Proceedings of the London Mathematical Society*.

Turing, Alan M. (1950), "Computing Machinery and Intelligence", *Mind*, Vol. 59, No. 236, pp. 433–460.

Turney, Peter and Patrick Pantel (2010), "From Frequency to Meaning: Vector Space Models of Semantics", *Journal of Artificial Intelligence Research*, Vol. 37, pp. 41–188.

Ulam, Stanisław (1958), "John von Neumann: 1903-1957", in J. C. Oxtoby, B. J. Pettis, and G. B. Price (eds.), *Bulletin of the Mathematical Society*, Vol. 64, No. 3, pp. 1–49.

Vaswani, Ashish, Noam Shazeer, Niki Parmar, Jakob Uszkoreit, Llion Jones, Aidan N. Gomez, Łukasz Kaiser, and Illia Polosukhin (2017), "Attention Is All You Need", *31st Conference on Neural Information Processing Systems* (NIPS).

Vinge, Vernor (1993), *The Coming Technological Singularity: How to Survive in the Post-Human Era*, NASA Technical Report.

Wang, Yongqiang, Yangyang Shi, Frank Zhang, Chunyang Wu, Julian Chan, Ching-Feng Yeh, and Alex Xiao (2021), "Transformer in Action: A Comparative Study of Transformer-Based Acoustic Models for Large Scale Speech Recognition Applications", *Proceedings of the International Conference on Acoustics, Speech, and Signal Processing (ICASSP)*, IEEE, pp. 6678-6782.

Warstadt, Alex and Samuel R. Bowman (2023), "What Artificial Neural Networks Can Tell Us about Human Language Acquisition", in Shalom Lappin and Jean-Philippe Bernardy (eds.), *Algebraic Structures in Natural Language*, Taylor and Francis, CRC Press, Boca Raton, FL and Oxford, pp. 17–59.

Way, Andy (2010), "Machine Translation", in Alexander Clark, Chis Fox, and Shalom Lappin (eds.), *The Handbook of Computational Linguistics and Natural Language Processing*, Wiley-Blackwell, Oxford, Hoboken, NJ, pp. 531–573.

Weiser, Benjamin (2023), "Here's What Happens When Your Lawyer Uses ChatGPT", *The New York Times*, May 27, 2023.

Weizenbaum, Joseph (1966), "ELIZA- A Computer Program for the Study of Natural Language Communication Between Man and Machine", *Communications of the ACM*, Vol. 9, No. 1, pp. 36–45.

Widrow, Bernard and Michael Lehrer (1990), "30 Years of Adaptive Neural Networks: Perceptron, Madaline, and Backpropagation", *Proceedings of the IEEE*, Vol. 78, No. 9, pp. 1415–1452.

Wilcox, Ethan G., Jon Gauthier, Jennifer Hu, Peng Qian, and Roger Levy (2023), "Learning Syntactic Structures from String Input", in Shalom Lappin and Jean-Philippe Bernardy (eds.), *Algebraic Structures in Natural Language*, Taylor and Francis, CRC Press, Boca Raton, FL and Oxford, pp. 113–137.

Woods, W. A. (1970), "Transition Network Grammars for Natural Language Analysis", *Communications of the ACM*, Vol. 13, No. 10, pp. 591–606.

Xu, Peng, Xiatian Zhu, and David A. Clifton (2023), "Multimodal Learning with Transformers: A Survey", *IEEE Transactions on Pattern Analysis and Machine Intelligence*, Vol. 45, No. 10. https://ieeexplore.ieee.org/document/10123038

Yang, Kaiyu, Aidan M. Swope, Alex Gu, Rahul Chalamala, Peiyang Song, Shixing Yu, Saad Godil, Ryan Prenger, and Anima Anandkumar (2023), "LeanDojo: Theorem Proving with Retrieval-Augmented Language Models", *37th Conference on Neural Information Processing Systems* NeurIPS.

Yudkowsky, Eliezer (2008), "Artificial Intelligence as a Positive and Negative Factor in Global Risk", in Nick Bostrom and Milan M. Ćirković (eds.), *Global Catastrophic Risks*, Oxford University Press, Oxford and New York, pp. 308–345.

Zadeh, Lotfi A. (1965), "Fuzzy Sets", *Information and Control*, Vol. 8, No. 3, pp. 338–353.

Zadeh, Lotfi A. (1975), "Fuzzy Logic and Approximate Reasoning", *Synthese*, Vol. 30, pp. 407–428.

Zhang, Hanqing, Haolin Song, Shaoyu Li, Ming Zhou, and Dawei Song (2023), "A Survey of Controllable Text Generation using Transformer-based Pre-trained Language Models", *ACM Computing Surveys*, Vol. 56, No. 3, article 64, pp. 1–37.

Zou, Leying and Warut Khern-am-nuai (2023), "AI and Housing Discrimination: The Case of Mortgage Applications", *AI and Ethics*, Vol. 3, pp. 1271–1281.

Index

Note: **Bold** page numbers refer to tables; *italic* page numbers refer to figures and page numbers followed by "n" denote endnotes.